LIQUID FLESH

Brenda Shaughnessy is an Okinawan-Irish American poet who grew up in Southern California. After graduating from the University of California, Santa Cruz, she moved to New York City where she received an MFA in Poetry from Columbia University and published her first book, *Interior with Sudden Joy* (Farrar, Straus & Giroux). Her five full-length collections include *The Octopus Museum* (Knopf, 2019), a *New York Times* Notable Book, and *Our Andromeda* (Copper Canyon Press, 2012), a finalist for the Griffin International Prize, the PEN/Open Book Award, and the Kingsley Tufts Prize. Her first UK publication, *Liquid Flesh: New & Selected Poems*, was published by Bloodaxe in 2022. Recipient of a 2018 Literature Award from the American Academy of Arts and Letters and a 2013 Guggenheim Foundation Fellowship, she is Professor of English at Rutgers University-Newark. She lives with her husband, the poet Craig Morgan Teicher, and their two children, in New Jersey.

Brenda Shaughnessy

LIQUID FLESH

NEW & SELECTED POEMS

BLOODAXE BOOKS

Copyright © Brenda Shaughnessy
1999, 2008, 2012, 2016, 2019, 2022

ISBN: 978 1 78037 629 5

First published 2022 by
Bloodaxe Books Ltd,
Eastburn,
South Park,
Hexham,
Northumberland NE46 1BS.

www.bloodaxebooks.com
For further information about Bloodaxe titles
please visit our website and join our mailing list
or write to the above address for a catalogue.

Supported using public funding by
**ARTS COUNCIL
ENGLAND**

Cover design: Neil Astley & Pamela Robertson-Pearce.

Printed in Great Britain by Bell & Bain Limited, Glasgow, Scotland, on
acid-free paper sourced from mills with FSC chain of custody certification.

ACKNOWLEDGEMENTS

Acknowledgements are due to the publishers of the five collections this selection draws upon. Poems from *Interior with Sudden Joy* by Brenda Shaughnessy, copyright © 1999 by Brenda Shaughnessy, reprinted by permission of Farrar, Straus and Giroux, all rights reserved. Poems from *Human Dark with Sugar* (2008), *Our Andromeda* (2012) and *So Much Synth* (2016) by permission of Copper Canyon Press. Poems from *The Octopus Museum* (2020) reprinted by permission of Alfred A. Knopf, a division of Penguin Random House.

The new poems are to be published in *Tanya*, a new collection by Brenda Shaughnessy, by Alfred A. Knopf in 2023 and appear here with their permission. 'The Impossible Lesbian Love Object(s)' was commissioned by MoMA (Museum of Modern Art). 'Tell Our Mothers We Tell Ourselves the Story We Believe Is Ours' was commissioned by National Museum of Norway for Laure Prouvost's 2022 exhibition in the Fredriksen Family Commission series. 'Who Sings Whose Songs?' and 'On "Loss of Feathers" by Ursula von Rydingsvard' was published in *Ways of Seeing: Writing on Drawings from the Jack Shear Collection* (The Drawing Center, 2021). 'The Poets are Dying' was published in *The New Yorker* on 28 October 2019. 'Moving Far Away' and 'What Have I Done?' are previously unpublished.

I would like to thank the editors of the original books in which many of these poems appeared: Deborah Garrison, Michael Wiegers and Jonathan Galassi. All my gratitude to Neil Astley for his vision, guidance, and brilliance. Special thanks go to Mira Braneck, Hilton Als, Jessica Rankin, Deborah Landau, Amy Key, Sarah Howe, my mother Mitsuko Higa, and my sister, Lisa. In loving memory of my father, Robert P. Shaughnessy (1945-2021).

CONTENTS

NEW POEMS

Interior with Sudden Joy

(1999)

Still Life, with Gloxinia

I will make something of you both pigment
and insecticide. Something natural,
even red, like serviceberries,
Which a cloister of young Benedictine
nuns, in exile and drought,
found and brilliantly crushed
into a blessed moxie wine.
With terrible pride, with gloxinia,
the slipper-shaped flower, served
it bitter and staining in the chalice.
By evening chapel, habits thrown up
and still, their insides found all blue,
as suspected. I am cold now and I cannot
paint or move you.

Lure, Lapse

There is no style in sleep,
only the sense of nethers startled
up from the supple interior.

Guarded handsomely, I am awake
(for a baker of course in love
with a painter will mix too hard)

and preening in the lord-loud and ecstatic doubt
purchased from all last nude cringing.

Dull bronze cowbells for hands
is what I want.

The serious honeycomb leaking,
I would streak you with yellow bruises.
Your garland, my shaky lamb,

we are close in this
slow evening gown,

we are growing down,
our winter-slung bodies fooled
and necklaced with furious morning.

Jouissance

Your phantoms hang neatly from skyhooks,
ready to be veils, ready to disembody you.

You have shelled yourself of this curved room
and the smell is of burnt door,

slackbelly, hot. It is an abattoir,
lacking its usual firmness.

Your ordinary sweet kinesis, peevish
in the crumble and whetstone of your body.

And so you go. Every city has a place called the Roxy.
Go. To keep from the quicksand of this:

Unbearable curl. Tender leviathan in the last
window, crimson facing west.

How could you? You are Gundella.
You are anyone's Maria.

Electric to perishing, your more auxiliary lovers,
like pralines or quaaludes, cannot touch you.

No teasing or lockjaw. Caustic. All of you, even shadow,
must be bull's-eye. Your shaggy, skeptical

quasar has died the way Andromeda dies:
so very late at night. You are disenchanted.

You are all rain-collected, in a butterfish sac
opaque and draining.

The description of this you hold under
like a genius in dark water.

What's Uncanny

is the body's wiry edge singed & dried,
touched at last by the curious

gloves of the question guard.
Too much choreography.

Hamstrings, half edible & music,
stretched like catgut, the sad-animal pull.

Our knees two peculiar systems
of locking, of looking. Too little dance.

Compulsion is always narcissism:
I miss you, admit it.

I'm gifted, I give in. I give you
all my old synesthetic fire.

Loved-body smoke is terribly popular
in dry neighborhoods,

and our lungs are succulents. We share
this loss of breathing. Listen for it.

Swell

Svelte with eventual sex, who could help
but gorge herself on low violet leaning everywhere?

The shine and shifting slate of the sky murmurs
its irresistible confession: *I am more than blue*

if you are the violent imprint. I am swollen,
vexed endlessly and only
finite against your bodies.

This slim stalk of silhouette slides via nimbus
down the eyelights without a skirmish.
Glossy with sly undoing, blisterlike.

We are disheveled, though too
skeptical to abandon our dimpled limbs

and fill the insides of slips with mere
threat and strop of thunderpeal.

We toss freely with fever this mirror
desilvered. And break into rain upon
finding such umber yielding of frost to febris.

This strumpet muscle under your breast describing
you minutely, *Volupt, volupt.*

Dear Gonglya,

The most inscrutable beautiful names in this world
always do sound like diseases.
It is because they are *engorged*.
G., I am a fool.
What we feel in the solar plexus wrecks us.
Halfway squatting on a crate where feeling happened. Caresses.

You know corporeal gifts besmirch thieves like me.
But she plucks a feather and my steam escapes.
                              We're awake
each night at pennymoon and we micro and necro.
I can't stop. But love and what-all:
the uncomfortable position of telling the truth,
like the lotus, can't be held long.
                              If she knew would she
just take all her favors from my marmalade
vessel and chuck them back
into the endless reversible garment which is my life—
                              an astonishing vanishing.
G., I know this letter is like a slice of elevator accident.
As smart folk would say,
'Everything is only Nothing's Truck.'

I would revise it and say that everything is only
nothing, truncated.

Love,

Your Igor

Rise

I can't believe you've come back,
like the train I missed so badly, barely,
which stopped & returned for me. It scared me,
humming backwards along the track.

I rise to make a supper succulent
for the cut of your mouth, your bite of wine
so sharp, you remember you were mine.
You may resist, you will relent.

At home in fire, desire is bread
whose flour, water, salt and yeast,
not yet confused, are still, at least,
in the soil, the sea, the mine, the dead.

I have all I longed for, you
in pleasure. You missed me, your body swelling.
Once more, you lie with me, smelling
of almonds, as the poisoned do.

Glossary

(of the body, performed in abstentia)

Appendix A: Irregular Verbs

Nursing:
>   The milk won the meat
> and the feet cheered.

Writing:
>   To bones, fat is only fog.

Whispering:
(see also *Secreting*)
>   Speckles furious at dots,
>   and all of them drunk in expensive boxes.

Nervous Throbbing:
>   The softest eggs, trembling for wax paper,
>   but a song would do.

Praying:
>   Peculiar remarks from a peripheral cousin.

Lying:
>   (down) When doing, no matter what else,
>   one cannot be the worst off in the world.

>   (little, white) Pressed essence of ham and corkboard.

Dreaming:
>   What is made from scrap sapphire
>   found lying around one's basement?

Begrudging:
>   A counterfeit fit.

Forgetting:
>   Boil feelers till soft, scrape off scorched
>   bits, put back in the head.

Trying:
>   I can never tell the truly gray heart, distracted as I am
>   by what is red about it.

Sexing:
>   Narrative Inclusion.

Writing:
>   The juice knife had its art cut, and ran.
>   (Example: I am made at you.)

Twisting:
>   (esp. ankle) Having pink, secure in the honey-only club,
>   but too dark to see by the moon so, insulted, rust.

Fingering:
>   Arms disarmed and explaining themselves.

Thinking:
>   Such truths are only perversions of the perfected false.
>   Plucked from the drink of a drunk heart.

Tonguing:
(see also *Writing*)
>   Enormous language smears your place.

Your One Good Dress

should never be light. That kind of thing feels
like a hundred shiny-headed waifs backlit
and skeletal, approaching. Dripping and in
unison, murmuring, 'We *are* you.'

No. And the red dress (think about it,
redress) is all neckhole. The brown
is a big wet beard with, of course, a backslit.
You're only as sick as your secrets.

There is an argument for the dull-chic,
the dirty olive and the Cinderelly. But those
who exhort it are only part of the conspiracy:
'Shimmer, shmimmer,' they'll say. 'Lush, shmush.'

Do not listen. It's a part of the anti-obvious
movement and it's sheer matricide. As your mum.
It would kill her if you were ewe gee el why.
And it's a crime to wonder, am I. In the dark a dare,

Am I now. You put on your Niña, your Pinta, your
Santa María. Make it simple to last your whole
life long. Make it black. Glassy or deep.
Your body is opium and you are its only true smoker.

This black dress is your one good dress.
Bury your children in it. Visit your pokey
hometown friends in it. Go missing for days.
Taking it off never matters. That just wears you down.

Lacquer

I found my mother's diary,
an indigo sack of silk and ink.
I read it. The words in Japanese
but the characters as American
as a girl of fashionable twelve
bearing an amnesia so dense
she could never drag it
out into the yard.

I couldn't tell you what
my mother's diary said.
That is private.
She would never tell me
that living always
with a husband's
language is like having
birthmarks on the pancreas.
Or that failing to persuade
daughters to sing open
her far invisible house
was an insomniac's mudwell,
an alien pox in the polished dark.

Epithalament

Other weddings are so shrewd on the sofa, short
and baffled, bassett-legged. All things

knuckled, I have no winter left, in my sore rememory,
to melt down for drinking water. Shrunk down.

Your wedding slides the way wiry dark hairs do, down
a swimming pool drain. So I am drained.

Sincerely. I wish you every chapped bird on this
pilgrimage to hold your hem up from the dust.

Dust is plural: infinite dust. I will sink in the sun,
I will crawl towards the heavy drawing

and design the curtains in the room
of never marrying you. Because it is a sinking,

because today's perfect weather is a later life's
smut. This soiled future unplans love.

I keep unplanning the same Sunday. Leg
and flower, breeze and terrier, I have no garden

and couldn't be happier. Please, don't lose me
here. I am sorry my clutch is all

tendon and no discipline: the heart is a severed
kind of muscle and alone.

I can hear yours in your room. I hear mine
in another room. In another's.

Cinema Poisoning

I will be your first, your thirst, your third.
I'll cramp up boxy, I will starlet out
in roads of light, or crimes, or words.
My second coming would not be allowed
unless your masokismet lifts her skirts.
So I will hold you flush against the glass.
Your voice & eye are muscle & they hurt
like prodigy too soft or quick in class.

My double agent, you would never ask
my miracles of sass & light to train
the athletes of seduction in the crass
voluptuary sciences like rain.

The sex & chess & cello fever's gone
from your myopic trust, my Avalon.

Postfeminism

There are two kinds of people, soldiers and women,
as Virginia Woolf said. Both for decoration only.

Now that is too kind. It's technical: virgins and wolves.
We have choices now. Two little girls walk into a bar,

one orders a shirley temple. Shirley Temple's pimp
comes over and says you won't be sorry. She's a fine

piece of work but she don't come cheap. Myself, I'm
in less fear of predators than of walking around

in my mother's body. That's sneaky, that's more
than naked. Let's even it up: you go on fuming in your

gray room. I am voracious alone. Blank and loose,
metallic lingerie. And rare black-tipped cigarettes

in a handmade basket case. Which of us weaves
the world together with a quicker blur of armed

seduction: your war-on-thugs, my body stockings.
Ascetic or carnivore. Men will crack your glaze

even if you leave them before morning. Pigs
ride the sirens in packs. Ah, flesh, technoflesh,

there are two kinds of people. Hot with mixed
light, drunk with insult. You and me.

Project for a Fainting

Oh, yes, the rain is sorry. Unfemale, of course, the rain is
with her painted face still plain and with such pixel you'd never see

it in the pure freckling, the lacquer of her. The world
is lighter with her recklessness, a handkerchief so wet it is clear.

To you. My withered place, this frumpy home (nearer
to the body than to evening) miserable beloved. I lie tender

and devout with insomnia, perfect on the center pillow past
midnight, sick with the thought of another year

of waking, solved and happy, it has never been this way! Believe
strangers who say the end is close for what could be closer?

You are my stranger and see how we have closed. On both ends.
Night wets me all night, blind, carried.

And watermarks. The plough of the rough on the slick,
love, a tendency toward fever. To break. To soil.

Would I dance with you? Both forever and rather die.
It would be like dying, yes. Yes I would.

I have loved the slaking of your forgetters, your indifferent
hands on my loosening. Through a thousand panes of glass

not at all transparent, and the temperature.
I felt that. What you say is not less than that.

You Love, You Wonder

You love a woman and you wonder where she goes all night in some tricked-
out taxicab, with her high heels and her corset and her big, fat mouth.

You love how she only wears her glasses with you, how thick
and cow-eyed she swears it's only ever you she wants to see.

You love her, you want her very ugly. If she is lovely big, you want her
scrawny. If she is perfect lithe, you want her ballooned, a cosmonaut.

How not to love her, her bouillabaisse, her orangina. When you took her
to the doctor the doctor said, 'Wow, look at that!' and you were proud,

you asshole, you love and that's how you are in love. Any expert, observing
human bodies, can see how she's exceptional, how she ruins us all.

But you really love this woman, how come no one can see this? Everyone must
become suddenly very clumsy at recognising beauty if you are to keep her.

You don't want to lose anything, at all, ever. You want her sex depilated, you
want everyone else not blind, but perhaps paralysed, from the eyes down.

You wonder where she goes all night. If she leaves you, you will know
everything about love. If she's leaving you now, you already know it.

Ever

Where, swift and wool in going?
Fell always wishing like this.

Tomorrow, want less and hunger bigger.
Fewer terror but stronger, staggered.

Taken heart outside to dry.
Rain surprise and ruined.

Silver cold and stops the swelling.
Why hurts from other body?

Why photo soothes with flat?
Salt soaks blood tender.

Brighten flesh in slap.
With word, not flood silent.

Not leave and take me
nowhere, swift and wool in going.

Interior with Sudden Joy

(after a painting by Dorothea Tanning)

To come into my room is to strike strange.
My plum velvet pillow & my hussy spot
the only furniture.

Red stripes around my ankles, tight
as sisters. We are maybe fourteen, priceless
with gooseflesh.

Our melon bellies, our mouths of tar. Us four:
my mud legged sister, my bunched-up self,
the dog & the whirligig just a prick on the eye.

We are all sewn in together, but the door is open.
The book is open too. You must write in red
like Jesus and his friends.

Be my other sister, we'll share a mouth.
We'll split the dress
down the middle, our home, our Caesarean.

When the Bishop comes he comes
diagonal, from the outside, & is a lie.
He comes to bless us all with cramps,

mole on the chin that he is,
to bring us the red something,
a glow, a pumping.

Not softly a rub with loincloth
& linseed. More of a beating,
with heart up the sleeve.

He says, *The air in here is tight & sore*
but punctured, sudden, by a string quartet.
We are! In these light-years we've wrung a star.

I am small for my age.
Child of vixenwood, lover of the color olive
and its stain.

I live to leave, but I never either.
One leg is so long we can all walk it.
Outside is a thousand bitten skins

and civilisation its own murder of crows.
I am ever stunned,
seduced whistle-thin

& hot with home. Breathless with
mercury, columbine. Come, let us miss
another wintertime.

Human Dark with Sugar

(2008)

I'm Over the Moon

I don't like what the moon is supposed to do.
Confuse me, ovulate me,

spoon-feed me longing. A kind of ancient
date-rape drug. So I'll howl at you, moon,

I'm angry. I'll take back the night. Using me to
swoon at your questionable light,

you had me chasing you,
the world's worst lover, over and over

hoping for a mirror, a whisper, insight.
But you disappear for nights on end

with all my erotic mysteries
and my entire unconscious mind.

How long do I try to get water from a stone?
It's like having a bad boyfriend in a good band.

Better off alone. I'm going to write hard
and fast into you, moon, face-fucking.

Something you wouldn't understand.
You with no swampy sexual

promise but what we glue onto you.
That's not real. You have no begging

cunt. No panties ripped off and the crotch
sucked. No lacerating spasms

sending electrical sparks through the toes.
Stars have those.

What do you have? You're a tool, moon.
Now, noon. There's a hero.

The obvious sun, no bullshit, the enemy
of poets and lovers, sleepers and creatures.

But my lovers have never been able to read
my mind. I've had to learn to be direct.

It's hard to learn that, hard to do.
The sun is worth ten of you.

You don't hold a candle
to that complexity, that solid craze.

Like an animal carcass on the road at night,
picked at by crows,

haunting walkers and drivers. Your face
regularly sliced up by the moving

frames of car windows. Your light is drawn,
quartered, your dreams are stolen.

You change shape and turn away,
letting night solve all night's problems alone.

Why Is the Color of Snow?

Let's ask a poet with no way of knowing.
Someone who can give us an answer,
another duplicity to help double the world.

What kind of poetry is all question, anyway?
Each question leads to an iceburn,
a snownova, a single bed spinning in space.

Poet, decide! I am lonely with questions.
What is snow? What isn't?
Do you see how it is for me.

Melt yourself to make yourself more clear
for the next observer.
I could barely see you anyway.

A blizzard I understand better,
the secrets of many revealed as one,
becoming another on my only head.

It's true that snow takes on gold from sunset
and red from rearlights. But that's occasional.
What is constant is white,

or is that only sight, a reflection of eyewhites
and light? Because snow reflects only itself,
self upon self upon self,

is a blanket used for smothering, for sleeping.
For not seeing the naked, flawed body.
Concealing it from the lover curious, ever curious!

Who won't stop looking.
White for privacy.
Millions of privacies to bless us with snow.

Don't we melt it?
Aren't we human dark with sugar hot to melt it?
Anyway, the question—

if a dream is a construction, then what
is not a construction? If a bank of snow
is an obstruction, then what is not a bank of snow?

A winter vault of valuable crystals
convertible for use only by a zen
sun laughing at us.

Oh Materialists! Thinking matter matters.
If we dream of snow, of banks and blankets
to keep our treasure safe forever,

what world is made, that made us that we keep
making and making to replace the dreaming at last.
To stop the terrible dreaming.

One Love Story, Eight Takes

Where you are tender, you speak your plural.
ROLAND BARTHES

1

One version of the story is I wish you back—
that I used each evening evening out
what all day spent wrinkling.

I bought a dress that was so extravagantly feminine
you could see my ovaries through it.

This is how I thought I would seduce you.
This is how frantic I hollowed out.

2

Another way of telling it
is to hire some kind of gnarled

and symbolic troll to make
a tape recording.

Of plastic beads coming unglued
fro a child's jewelry box.

This might be an important sound,
like serotonin or mighty mitochondria,

so your body hears about
how you stole the ring made

from a glittery opiate
and the locket that held candy.

3

It's only fair that I present yet another side,
as insidious as it is,

because two sides hold up nothing but each other.

A tentacled skepticism,
a suspended contempt,

such fancies and toxins form a third wall.

A mean way to end
and I never dreamed we meant it.

4

Another way of putting it is like
slathering jam on a scrape.

Do sweets soothe pain or simply make it stick?
Which is the worst! So much technology
and no fix for sticky if you can't taste it.

I mean there's no relief unless.
So I'm coming, all this excitement,

to your house. To a place where there's no room for play.
It is possible you'll lock me out and I'll finally
focus on making mudcakes that look solid in the rain.

5

In some cultures the story told is slightly different—
in that it is set in an aquarium and the audience participates

as various fish. The twist comes when it is revealed
that the most personally attractive fish have eyes

only on one side and repel each other like magnets.
The starfish is the size of an eraser and does as much damage.

Starfish, the eponymous and still unlikely hero, has
those five pink moving suckerpads

that allow endless permutations so no solid memory,
no recent history, nothing better, left unsaid.

6

The story exists even when there are no witnesses,
kissers, tellers. Because secrets secrete,

and these versions tend to be slapstick, as if in a candy
factory the chocolate belted down the conveyor too fast

or everyone turned sideways at the same time by accident.
This little tale tries so hard to be humorous,

wants so badly to win affection and to lodge.
Because nothing is truly forgotten *and* loved.

7

Three million Richards can't be wrong.
So when they levy a critique of an undertaking which,

in their view, overtakes, I take it seriously.
They think one may start a tale off whingey

and wretched in a regular voice.
But when one strikes out whimsically,

as if meta-is-betta, as if *it isn't you,*
as if this story is *happening to nobody*

it is only who you are fooling that's nobody.
The Richards believe you cannot

privately jettison into the sky, just for fun.
You must stack stories from the foundation up.

From the sad heart and the feet tired of supporting it.
Language is architecture, after all, not an air capsule,

not a hang glide. This is real life.
So don't invite anyone to a house that hasn't been built.

Because no one unbuilds meticulously
and meticulously is what allows hearing.

Three million Richards make one point.
I hear it in order to make others. Mistakes.

8

As it turns out, there is a wrong way to tell this story.
I was wrong to tell you how multi-true everything is,

when it would be truer to say nothing.
I've invented so much and prevented more.

But, I'd like to talk with you about other things,
in absolutely quiet. In extreme context.

To see you again, isn't love revision?
It could have gone so many ways.

This just one of the ways it went.
Tell me another.

I'm Perfect at Feelings,

so I have no problem telling you
why you cried over the third lost
metal or the mousetrap. I knew
that orgasms weren't your fault
and that feeling of keeping solid
in yourself but wanting an ecstatic
black hole was just bad beauty.

Certain loves were perfect
in the daytime and had
every right to express carnally behind
the copy machine and there are
no hard feelings for the boozy
sodomy and sorry XX daisy chain,
whenever it felt right for you.

And when the moment of soft
levitation with erasing hands
made you feel dirty, like
the main person to think up love
in the first place, I knew that.
It's okay, you're an innocent
with the brilliance of an animal

stuffing yourself sick on a kill.
Don't, don't feel like the runt alien
on my ship: I get you. I know
the dimensions of your wishing
and losing and don't think you
a glutton with petty beefs. But
even I, who know your triggers,

your emblematic sacs of sad fury,
I understand why the farthest fat trees
sliver down with your disappointment

and why the big sense of the world,
wrong before you, shrugs but
somewhere grasps your spinning,
stunning, alone. But you have me.

Drift

I'll go anywhere to leave you but come with me.
All the cities are like you anyway. Windows
darken when I get close enough to see.
Any place we want to stay's polluted,

the good spots taken already by those
who ruin them. And restaurants we'd never find.
We'd run a ditch by a river in nights
so long they must be cut by the many pairs

of wrong-handled scissors maybe god owns
and doesn't share. I water god.
I make a haunted lake and rinse and rinse.
I take what I want, and have ever since what

I want disappeared, like anything hunted,
That's what you said. Disappointment
isn't tender, dried and wide instead.
The tourists snapped you crying,

and the blanket I brought was so dirty
it must have been lying around
in lice and blood that whole year we fought.
It wasn't clear, so I forgot.

I haven't been sleeping, next to you
twitching to bury my boring eyes,
The ship made you sad, and the ferry, and canoe.
All boats do.

Me in Paradise

Oh, to be ready for it, unfucked, ever-fucked.
To have only one critical eye that never
divides a flaw from its lesson.

To play without shame. To be a woman
who feels only the pleasure of being used
and who reanimates the user's

anguished release in a land
for the future to relish, to buy
new tights for, to parade in fishboats.

To scare up hope without fear of hope,
not holding the hole, I will catch
the superbullet in my throat

and feel its astounding force
with admiration. Absorbing its kind
of glory. I must be someone

with very short arms to have lost you,
to be checking the windows
of the pawnshop renting space in my head,

which pounds with all the clarity
of a policeman on my southernmost door.
To wish and not jinx it: to wish

and not fish for it: to wish and forget it.
To ratchet myself up with hot liquid
and find a true surprise.

Prowling the living room for the lightning,
just one more shock,
to bring my slow purity back.

To miss you without being so damn cold
all the time. To hold you without dying otherwise.
To die without losing death as an alternative.

To explode with flesh, without collapse.
To feel sick in my skeleton, in all the serious
confetti of my cells, and know why.

Loving you has made me so scandalously
beautiful. To give myself to everyone but you.
To luck out of you. To make any other mistake.

Embarrassment

It's a wave, isn't it? Not a particle.
A fresh, cool wave, so why am I flushed
and not washed?
Why dirtier than before?

1 *Etymology*

On the subject of our names.
They're so embracing,
thinking they're all us

and swallowing themselves
into our nausea.

Yet we never quite die on the spot.
We put off being what we're called,
we take the hint.

Time is never wasted.
It is always spent.

2 *Teleology*

Sheer fabric trailing through 4 a.m.
I thought it was opaque and earlier.

3 *Mathematics*

I know you know I know.
And the mirror multiplies inside.

The world is no bigger, but next time
do the math,

because I wanted to know none
of what I now know twice.

4 *The Principle of the Borg*

Saying 'There's no one like me'
accomplishes the exact opposite
of what you mean.

It is true only insofar as it is true
for everyone equally.

So it means you are not special
in any way. Which should be enough for you.

5 *Documentary*

This clothing, a maladaptive wrapping,
cuts me up. I am a vignette,

floated knowingly
since I pulled myself through myself,

like a unitard. Too many eyeholes

have been cut and pieced together
to make flesh less various with others.

6 *Medicine*

The cure for embarrassment
is substitution.

Strap, don't pluck.
Baldness makes headlines.

Use grass. Use less.
Shorts under your skirt for recess.

Redo the surfaces of your wrong turns to make
taking them smoother in the future.

7 *Cosmology*

Things are less embarrassing
at the cellular level. Remember?

We were a whole part of the universe
before Mother busted the party.

Before we were ourselves.
Now, like dirty soap, we

attract what we repel.

8 *Apology*

Even the clumsiest fate is perfectly shaped,
so the view took over looking

but the sweetest thing I've ever known
is obscene with a beautiful

sugar rotted down to its truth.

Loving you a serious accidental shame
and day flatulates into night,

trips and falls in front of millions
into morning.

In thrall to this pocus:
the end of fear starts

with such an annihilating blush,
with such a stutter.

A Poet's Poem

If it takes me all day,
I will get the word *freshened* out of this poem.

I put it in the first line, then moved it to the second,
and now it won't come out.

It's stuck. I'm so frustrated,
so I went out to my little porch all covered in snow

and watched the icicles drip, as I smoked
a cigarette.

Finally I reached up and broke a big, clear spike
off the roof with my bare hand.

And used it to write a word in the snow.
I wrote the word *snow*.

I can't stand myself.

First Date and Still Very, Very Lonely

A pleasant, leather poison
is the trick to smelling
good to female saddles,

that is, saddles with a hole
and not a pommel. Remember
those? Gone the way

of vestal virgins and tight,
white black holy hell and with it,
the lesbian Elysium of old.

I miss the idea of wives.
The loving circle.
But onward. Today

is a sacred day. A date day.
An exception to the usual
poor me, poor me!

I'm not poor and I'm not me.
I remember both
states as soon ago as last week.

But that's history.
That is different. At a party,
once, everyone was so careful

that only I cut my lip drinking
from the winterspring,
a kind of cold, decorative trough

centerpiece we were all
drinking from. The idea is
you're like animals.

If you ask, about the cut, *Why me?*
The answer is, *Of course me.*
In what world ever possible not *me?*

I could admit that with open blood
running down my chin
like hyena butter or gasoline.

I was mortified, really lost.
After that I thought,
I have to meet someone.

Dancing in My Room Alone

I could be an eel in whirled stillwaters,
the semiotic blue of trick quicksand,
meaningless and true.

In my room, ordinary yellow objects
like lapel labels and plates
smile like smilies,

caressed like air in movies,
the texture of froth. I need sugar.
Need it like a right, so sugar

is given. A river of high
minutes rising to a horizon,
only ever seeing my double eyes.

I'm so really truly enough
that I should save myself for later.
Later, don't come now.

Don't turn me back into that seventh-
grader in a human ring around the gym,
certain I'm not in the circle.

Now I'm slinging room-darkness
to sun. Swelling hips
incredibly undone,

my blind blood singing,
'qua aqua aqua',
intoxicated

with this song's cologne,
a silk ribbon of paint
driven through nature.

Fun, who knew? Spinning
with nothing, as earth does,
I flew more than I could lose.

O god of ether, god of vapor,
I could use one of either of you.
Take me as a swan would.

Take me, wing me up and make me
dance, impaled on a hooked
prick of cyclone.

Sightless. Wind my limbs, digits
clutching feathers, around you,
and disappear.

I won't fall. I know how to do it now.
I broke the window with god's ball.
I am smoothly used

and honeyed, self-twinned, fearless,
a wineskin emptying
into a singing stranger.

A Brown Age

Summer took every one of my
dresses while I was having
them perfumed;

summer wore them every day
so I was naked and living in a cave
where frugivores

snuffled in the melonflesh.
I wrote you a letter in dirty ink.
Asking you here.

Why not? Trees move
at least as much as we do,
if only their heads and arms.

I didn't write that.
I scratched it
on a rock and skipped the rock.

Brownie, the pink oranges are hanging
just behind your head.
It's the life you can't see.

If I turned your head, you'd still
only see the turning.
Not fruit. Not me.

But legs moved to prove you came
at all. At last, we were sleeping
and fucking and it was fall.

Now in the dark brown dark,
it's cold and white.
Your eyes are largely

plural like fish
sleepfloating in their zones,
no souls, but thirsty.

On the mouth of the cave,
there is an icicle that had no way
here in summer.

Now it melts down
and refreezes into the shape
of a wishbone or two wet

legs to escape on. I will break
them both and put it all in a cup.
I'll wish for water,

that is, waste a wish on what
will already come.
Please don't leave.

Please drink it. I'm waiting
for noon to become midnight
and for you to drink it.

Our Andromeda

(2012)

Artless

is my heart. A stranger
berry there never was,
tartless.

Gone sour in the sun,
in the sunroom or moonroof,
roofless.

No poetry. Plain. No
fresh, special recipe
to bless.

All I've ever made
with these hands
and life, less

substance, more rind.
Mostly rim and trim,
meatless

but making much smoke
in the old smokehouse,
no less.

Fatted from the day,
overripe and even
toxic at eve. Nonetheless,

in the end, if you must
know, if I must bend,
waistless,

to that excruciation.
No marvel, no harvest
left me speechless,

yet I find myself
somehow with heart,
aloneless.

With heart,
fighting fire with fire,
flightless.

That loud hub of us,
meat stub of us, beating us
senseless.

Spectacular in its way,
its way of not seeing,
congealing dayless

but in everydayness.
In that hopeful haunting
(a lesser

way of saying
in darkness) there is
silencelessness

for the pressing question.
Heart, what art you?
War, star, part? Or less:

playing a part, staying apart
from the one who loves,
loveless.

Head Handed

Stop belonging to me so much, face-head.
Leave me to my child and my flowers.

I can't run with you hanging on to me like that.
It's like having ten dogs on a single lead

and no talent for creatures.
No hands, no trees. Not my dogs, nobody's.

Don't you have a place to go, face-head?
Deep into the bring basement of another life?

To kill some time, I mean. That furnace
light could take a shine to you.

There are always places, none of them mine.
And always time—rainbow sugar show

of jimmies falling from ice cream's sky—
but that stuff's extra, it's never in supply.

'Never,' however, acres of it. Violet beans
and sarcasm. Too many flavors of it.

All those prodigal particles,
flimsily whimsical miracles, an embarrassment

of glitches. The chorus just *more us*.
But nowhere bare and slippery have I

got a prayer. If I had two hands
to rub together I wouldn't waste the air.

Nemesis

The sun has its nemesis, evil twin star,
not its opposite but its spirit,
undead angel,

extra life. Another version.
The Andromeda Galaxy bears children
who become us, year after ancient,

ridiculous year. The children,
the alternatively filled selves unrecognisable
to our faeries, our animals and gods:

us utterly replaced.
The kids we were, rejected like organs
donated to the wrong body.

Why aren't they dear to us?
Why is that child least loved
by is own grown self?

If you aren't me then be banished from me,
weird orphan with limp and lisp.
Who, nameless brainsake, are you?

Not my substance or my shadow
but projectile vomit, a noxious gas.
Don't be me, please don't be me,

says the adult, looking back into wormhole
as if jumping into foxhole.
Not me, never again: that terrible child

with the insufferable littlesoul
and bad mom and sameself sister,
and balky, stalky brother

and monotone uncle and messed-with cousins,
and let's not ever talk about the father,
the fater, pater, hated, fattened, late, latter dad.

Perhaps the Andromedans are such early
versions of us we can't hate yet, ghosts
or our pre-living selves, earliest babies.

Perhaps they're only life*like*, like
a robot cook or a motion detector,
not like a dog we love and know,

or claim to know,
who nonetheless attacks grandma
somehow. We say so, said so, toldya so.

That's what you get for believing in aliens,
for replacing our earhorn of plenty
with a megaphone of corpsedust.

Listen, it's moving closer, the Andromeda
Galaxy, this other us, this museum of mucus
and keyboards and keyboard fingertip records

that their governments are already optimised
to keep post-digitally. All of which looks
much more like a craps game to us, a hinky

life-filler, time-killer, the best selection of credit
card pill extensions with rapid-release hypo-air
no one but addicts can tolerate.

Only 2.5 million light-years away, lessening
daily, and that's collapsible
space, of course, made of light. Just flip

the switch and poof. We're there.
The space, then, the dog-run-sized length
between the golden retriever

and the Labrador retriever,
isn't so much space as time, and since time
is breath…well. Take a deep one.

We have all day, as a matter of objective fact.
Slip on a glossy patch of antimatter
and I've inhaled my unutterable

opposite of potential self, smeared out
the tracing of my nemesis: Olympic
gymnast teen me or seventh-grade best friend

Shannon, or the cricket-eating
self-sister with the spiny-belled name I dream
at night and call out but can't ever know

in this world. Such a thing is called a soul?
A personality? Sometimes diagnosed 'possession'?
Nemesis, namesake, nevermore.

O funny other self,
how I long to know you! You were ingested
so easily, absorbed like a lotion

in the desert. Even in the evening.
For there are no light years. Years are heavy.
There is only light. It never bends:

that's the property it mortgaged in order
to pick up speed. But parallel lines can meet
just like that if someone breaks the rules.

Some criminal sharing my name
or an alien name sharing my crime.
The rules are there are no rules. Lingua franca.

Isn't the space between what is
and what coulda woulda Buddha been,
that same space between short skull

and long face, that oiled jaw hinged
for supple expression, for saying
and blaming and braying and allaying

and naming: *I this* not *I that*, tit not tat,
want not waste, and *yes* not *yes, but...*
What your mother

tells you over and over to shut,
to smile, first to not talk to strangers
and then be kind to them.

To sponsor the tail of another winner's
horse. To Go for It.
To become something in this life.

But once the gardenias
are floating in seawater for the themed gala
of your body, this special night,

they are dying, bacteria or no bacteria,
life against life, this world
butted up against the next.

Simultaneity aside, we are all next.
All go to the light.
Heavily, with our childhoods we go.

I'll go with my stars,
and my sorry body, stranger
to myself, will say go.

The World's Arm

A strong, pale wind on the thighs,
it was no seaspray, no AC,

but cold mnemonic, a breath
of spotless decision,

a kind of bulk, a true surface
thickened by foreign pears

as if winter brought us its fruit
first to me for approval

before it let December
fill its basket to capacity.

I spoke too calmly for one
who didn't believe in anything.

Mouth full of pears,
full of promises I'd no way

to speak, much less keep, I tended
to gesture towards a Universal

Field of Grass, hoping to break
as many blades as my wide self

could in one pass. One pass—
but we're wasted with feeling,

breathing funny and stuck rough
like an IV into a paralysed arm.

And that's the World's Arm
that can't write anymore,

or sign its name, or pick
the thickness from the trees.

My fingerprints transform
into proboscis, by degrees.

Streetlamps

The unplowed road is unusable
unless there's no snow.

But in dry, warm weather,
it's never called an unplowed road.

To call it so, when it isn't so,
doesn't make it so, though it is so

when it snows and there's no plow.
It's a no-go. Let's stay inside.

And here we are again:
no cake without breaking

eggs, unless it's a vegan cake
in which there are never any eggs

only the issue, the question,
the primacy of eggs,

which remains even in animal-free
foods, eaten by animal-free

humans in an inhumane world, lit
with robots breathing

powerlessly in nature.
O streetlamp,

wallflower clairvoyant,
you are so futuristically

old-fashioned,
existing in the daytime

for later, because it becomes
later eventually, then

earlier, then later again.
And a place is made

for that hope, if I call
it hope when half the time

is erased by the other half.
Light becomes itself

in the dark, and becomes
nothing when the real light

comes. It is enough to make
even the simplest organism

insane. Why did the chicken
cross the unplowed road?

Because it was trying
to beat the egg to the other side.

It wanted to be first,
at last, and to stay first,

at least until the day
breaks itself sunny side,

and the rooster crows.
The only snows are dark snows.

Liquid Flesh

In a light chocolatine room
with blackout windows,
a loud clock drowns in soft dawn's

syllables, crisscrossed
with a broken cloudiness
I'd choose as my own bedcovers

but cannot. My choice of sleep
or sky has no music of its own.
There's no 'its own' while the baby cries.

Oh, the baby cries. He howls and claws
like a wrongly minor red wolf
who doesn't know his mother.

I know I am his mother, but I can't
quite click on the word's essential aspects,
can't denude the flora

or disrobe the kind of housecoat
'mother' always is. Something
cunty, something used.

Whatever meaning the word itself
is covering, like underwear,
that meaning is so mere and meager

this morning. Mother. Baby.
Chicken and egg. It's so obnoxious
of me: I was an egg

who had an egg
and now I'm chicken,
as usual scooping up

both possibilities,
or what I used to call
possibilities. I used

to be this way, so ontologically
greedy, wanting to be it all.
Serves me right.

My belief in the fluidity
of the self turns out to mean
my me is a flow of wellwater,

without the well, or the bucket,
a hole dug and seeping.
A kind of unwell, where

the ground reabsorbs
what it was displaced to give.
The drain gives meaning to the sieve.

As I said: a chicken who still
wants to be all potential.
Someone who springs

and falls, who cannot see
how many of us I have
in me—and I do not like them all.

Do I like us? Can I love us?
If anyone comes
first it's him, but how can that be?

I was here way, way first.
I have the breasts, godawful, and he
the lungs and we share the despair.

For we are a we, aren't we? We split
a self in such a way that there isn't
enough for either of us.

The father of the baby is sleepy
and present in his way, in the way
of fathers. He is devoted like

few fathers and maybe hurts
like I hurt, like no fathers.
I don't know what someone else

feels, not even these someones
who are also me. Do they hurt
like I do? Why can't they

tell me, or morse or sign: let
me know they know where and how
and why it hurts? Or something?

What is the point of other people,
being so separate, if we can't
help a person get that pain

will stick its shiv into anything,
just to get rid of the weapon
and because it can? For if we share

ourselves then they, too, must
also be in so much pain.
I can hear it. Oh, my loves.

The wood of the crib, the white
glow of the milk (which must
have siphoned off the one

and only pure part of me, leaving
me with what, toxicity
or sin or mush?), the awful softness.

I've been melted into something
too easy to spill. I make more
and more of myself in order

to make more and more of the baby.
He takes it, this making. And somehow
he's made more of me, too.

I'm a mother now.
I run to the bathroom, run
to the kitchen, run to the crib

and I'm not even running.
These places just scare up as needed,
the wires that move my hands

to the sink, to the baby,
to the breast are electrical.
I'm in shock.

One must be in shock to say so,
as if one's own state is assessable,
like a car accident or Minnesota taxes.

A total disaster, this sack of liquid
flesh which yowls and leaks
and I'm talking about me

not the baby. Me, this puddle
of a middle, this utilised vessel,
cracked hull, divine

design. It's how it works. It's how
we all got here. Deform
following the function...

But what about me? I whisper
secretly and to think,
around these parts used to be

the joyful place of sex,
what is now this intimate
terror and squalor.

My eyes burned out at three a.m. and again
at six and eleven. This is why the clock
is drowning, as I said earlier.

I'm trying to explain it.
I repeat myself, or haven't I already?
Tiny self, alone with a tiny self.

I'll say it: he hurt me, this new
babe, then and now.
Perhaps he always will,

though thoughts of the future
seem like science fiction novels
I never finished reading.

Their ends like red nerves
chopped off by cleaver, not aliens,
this very moment, saving nothing for later.

He howls with such fury and clarity
I must believe him.
No god has the power

to make me believe anything,
yet I happen to know
this baby knows a way out.

This dark hole closing in on me
all around: he'll show me
how to get through

the shock and godlessness
and the rictus of crushed flesh,
into the rest of my life.

Visitor

I am dreaming of a house just like this one

but larger and opener to the trees, nighter

than day and higher than noon, and you,

visiting, knocking to get in, hoping for icy

milk or hot tea or whatever it is you like.

For each night is a long drink in a short glass.

A drink of blacksound water, such a rush

and fall of lonesome no form can contain it.

And if it isn't night yet, though I seem to

recall that it is, then it is not for everyone.

Did you receive my invitation? It is not

for everyone. Please come to my house

lit by leaf light. It's like a book with bright

pages filled with flocks and glens and groves

and overlooked by Pan, and that seductive satyr

in whom the fish is also cooked. A book that

took too long to read but minutes to unread—

that is—to forget. Strange are the pages

thus. Nothing but the hope of company.

I made too much pie in expectation. I was

hoping to sit with you in a treehouse in a

nightgown in a real way. Did you receive

my invitation? Written in haste, before

leaf blinked out, before the idea fully formed.

An idea like a stormcloud that does not spill

or arrive but moves silently in a direction.

Like a dark book in a long life with a vague

hope in a wood house with an open door.

Karaoke Realness at the Love Hotel

At the microphone, suddenly—oh no—
is Sandra the Available,

in her endless yellow dress
and award-winning earrings,

about to sing Rose Dickey's unrecorded
cakewreck of a hybrid poemsong,

'Sheep Child o' Mine.'
Now watch her win the night

before it's all over. She's no loser
with a fever but no lover.

Not like me. I live in a hotel
with no rooms, just a lobby and lifts

leading to experiences.
Time to ask another person,

someone who's been outside
the fishbowl long enough

to wonder if there will ever again
be enough water. Rat race,

hamster wheel, dog run.
(Okay, dog run's different.

It's not for people.)
I'm not a real people-person.

Just like reality is not really realness,
people. Just try and point out to me

what's not fake or paste or false?
Or trick or replica

or denial or dream or drama
or simulation or reenactment

or knockoff or artificial, a ruse,
a work of art, illusion,

a lie, a mistake, fantasy,
a misconception, missed-connection,

delusion, hallucination,
insincere, invalid or invented,

a rehearsal with no performance?
A viable world with no excuse to exist?

In my hotel the sleep is free.
In any hotel. Why shouldn't it be?

And that old girl Sandra?
Turns out she can really sing.

Products of Perception

Perhaps an implantation.
Perhaps there is no soul. And biotech
and metaphysics can't prove I'm whole.

If there were clear demarcation
between me and *why me*
then why wine and why whine

and if so, why not all the time?
Since flavor is olfactory
and pleasure in the brain,

does it make sense for the mouth
to open and admit blame?
Fluid body, fluent tongue,

flu-like symptoms hide a hole
through which a neutered fever catches
neutered cold. I'm told a kind of eerie light

flicks on when mind becomes itself.
Like when a book is opened,
and read, or just falls off the shelf.

Miracles

I spent the whole day
crying and writing, until
they became the same,

as when the planet covers the sun
with all its might and still
I can see it, or when one dead

body gives its heart
to a name on a list. A match.
A light. Sailing a signal

flare behind me for another to find.
A scratch on the page
is a supernatural act, one twisting

fire out of water, blood out of stone.
We can read us. We are not alone.

Big Game

(after Richard Brautigan's 'A CandleLion Poem')

What began as wildfire ends up
on a candlewick. In reverse,
it is contained,

a lion head in a hunter's den.
Big Game.

Bigger than one I played
with matches and twigs and glass
in the shade.

When I was young, there was no sun
and I was afraid.

Now, in grownhood, I call the ghost
to my fragile table, my fleshy supper,
my tiny flame.

Not just any old but the ghost,
the last one I will be,

the future me,
finally the sharpest knife
in the drawer.

The pride is proud.
The crowd is loud, like garbage dumping

or how a brown bag ripping
sounds like a shout
that tells the town the house

is burning down.
Drowns out some small folded breath

of otherlife: O that of a lioness licking
her cubs to sleep
in a dream of savage gold.

O that roaring, not yet and yet
and not yet dead.

So many fires start in my head.

I Wish I Had More Sisters

I wish I had more sisters,
enough to fight with and still
have plenty more to confess to,
embellishing the fight so that I
look like I'm right and then turn
all my sisters, one by one, against
my sister. One sister will be so bad
the rest of us will have a purpose
in bringing her back to where
it's good (with us) and we'll feel
useful, and she will feel loved.

Then another sister
will have a tragedy, and again,
we will unite in our grief, judging
her much less than we did the bad
sister. This time it was not
our sister's fault. This time
it could have happened to any
of us and in a way it did. We'll
know she wasn't the only
sister to suffer. We all suffer
with our choices, and we
all have our choice of sisters.

My sisters will seem like a bunch
of alternate me, all the ways
I could have gone. I could see
how things pan out without
having to do the things myself.
The abortions, the divorces,
the arson, swindles, poison jelly.
But who could say they weren't
myself, we are so close. I mean,
who can tell the difference?

I could choose to be a fisherman's
wife since I'd be able to visit
my sister in her mansion, sipping
bubbly for once, braying
to the others who weren't invited.
I could be a traveler, a seer,
a poet, a potter, a flyswatter.
None of those choices would be
as desperate as they seem now.
My life would be like one finger
on a hand, a beautiful, usable, ringed,
wrung, piano-and-dishpan hand.

There would be both more and less
of me to have to bear. None of us
would be forced to be stronger
than we could be. Each of us could
be all of us. The pretty one.
The smart one. The bitter one.
The unaccountably-happy-
for-no-reason one. I could be,
for example, the hopeless
one, and the next day my sister
would take my place, and I would
hold her up until my arms gave way
and another sister would relieve me.

Magi

If only you'd been a better mother.

How could I have been a better mother?
I would have needed a better self,
and that is a gift I never received.

So you're saying it's someone else's fault?

The gift of having had a better mother myself,
my own mother having had a better mother herself.
The gift that keeps on not being given.

Who was supposed to give it?

How am I supposed to know?

Well, how am I supposed to live?

I supposed you must live as if you had been
given better to live with. Comb your hair, for instance.

I cut off my hair, to sell for the money
to buy you what you wanted.

I wanted nothing but your happiness.

I can't give you that!
What would Jesus do?
He had a weird mother too...

Use the myrrh, the frankincense, as if
it were given unconditionally, your birthright.

It's a riddle.

All gifts are a riddle, all lives are
in the middle of mother-lives.

But it's always winter in this world.
There is no end to ending.

The season of giving, the season
when the bears are never cold,
because they are sleeping.

The bears are never cold, Mama,
but I am one cold, cold bear.

At the Book Shrink

one learns to say 'My body uses me
as a grape uses wine'—

to talk about inevitability,
the essence of plot.

But what happens when a person
understands she is being sent

back, glass by glass,
to the invisible pouring stations

of the larger narrative?
That she is merely like or likely

a person in a book?
Like a saltwater balloon

sinking in the ocean.
Like a person in a book, like

I said already. Someone's
not listening. Someone's

eating breakfast or falling
asleep or texting a married lover

as shrinks are wont to do.
If I am boring then at least

I am getting somewhere:
through the wood I knock on.

My story is telling.
But it's not telling *me*.

I need help getting to the next part.
When I open my mouth,

liquid rushes in, endrunkening.
When I close it,

dark, secret-looking drops spill
crimson on the page.

Headlong

Be strange to yourself,
in your love, your grief.

Your wet eyelashes a black
fringe on brown pain

and your feet unbelievably
sure, somehow, surfing

your own shadow,
that too-large one cresting

just now, too soon for you
to get inside the curl:

the one place in the ocean
where it's safe. And safe

only for a half-breath
(a fish's sip with
hooked lip),

only for that one blink
of an eye already shut (tiptoe

to the foreshadow) against
the headlong wall of salt water.

The New People

I had no desire to get to know the screamers,
our loud-in-ten-ways, annoying, drunk and boorish
neighbors, but I didn't put up

a fence or anything. Didn't fight it
when they brought us plates of their fatty meals
and overlong chitchat. We were new,

just renting, and I didn't want to be rude,
either, when Joanna and Vince
brought us their statue of the Virgin Mary

when our newborn son was in the hospital.
Joanna had tears in her eyes and though I am not
Catholic, or even Christian—or not

anymore, anyway, I think, if it's like what I suppose
in that you have to keep up with the dues
to stay in the club—

I accepted the statue. I took in the alien
mother and wrapped her in a blanket.
I lay her on a low shelf and broke

the news to my Jewish husband, who cringed
and said, 'She gave you *what?*'
But I didn't care

what it was, from what god or goddess
or neighbor or creature or kiln.
I was becoming someone I didn't know

each day without my little boy—near insanity
without his tiny, pure, hurt self. All those wires.
Blessed Virgin Mary, Mother of God,

Holy Statue in my baby's silent room, I promise
I will believe in you, and in Jesus, too. Please...
Why was I cradling a 'mother' statue,

a ceramic doll, this creepy relic,
instead of my living, beautiful son?
If she could make it all the way here,

across so many territories of indifference,
into my most secret empty room—
surely my child, who belonged, would come home soon?

Nachträglichkeit

(after Kaja Silverman's 'Flesh of My Flesh')

On having slashed myself from throat to instep
in one unbroken line,

I suppose it was a reenactment, Freud's *Nachträglichkeit*:
the second act. The past presses so hard

on the present, the present is badly bruised,
blood brims under the skin.

That was the situation I was in. Wearing a jacket of blood
from an earlier crime,

which was also mine. A curving zipper with misaligned
teeth, open to show red lipstick,

meat. And a stage smile, have a seat! Normally I'm much
more careful, naturally something

like this would only ever happen in a dream,
but even dreams have their dreams

of finding their dreamer awake, silent within earshot,
carving knife in hand.

Did you know that anguish things the blood and thickens
the vessel? It was like cutting

a rare steak. A minotaur, glittering with rubies
and pink candles. My hands hung

like electrical wires off a building on the edge of collapse,
every one of my gestures symbolic,

ruined of magic. For there is no miraculous beast,
and there never was, standing

on the golden field of frozen honey clover,
each leaf strong enough to bend

under everything's weight. Strong because it bends.
Because it has already been crushed,

but its cells know that blight, one massive cut,
will slit each tiny skin surgically

in order to save the field from itself. I cannot suffer
the same fate twice, force my own hand

or stay it. Can't repeat or unrepeat. This finitude
is infinite and infinitely expanding.

Our Andromeda

When we get to Andromeda, Cal,
you'll have the babyhood you deserved,
all the groping at light sockets

and putting sand in your mouth
and learning to say *Mama* and *I want*
and sprinting down the yard

as if to show me how you were leaving
me for the newest outpost of Cal.
You'll get the chance to walk

without pain, as if such a thing
were a matter of choosing a song
over a book, of napping at noon

instead of fighting it. You'll have
the chance to fight every nap,
every grown-up decision that bugs

you, and it will be a fair fight, this time,
Cal, in Andromeda. You will win.

*

In Andromeda there would be no
sleepy midwife who doesn't know
her own weakness, no attending

nurse who defers like a serf
to the sleepy midwife, no absent
obstetrician, no fetal heart monitor

broken and ignored, no sloppy
hospital where everyone checks
their own boxes and only consults

the check marks when making
decisions that will hurt us, Cal.
None of those individual segments

will be there in Andromeda,
no segments to constitute the worm
that burrowed into our own bodies

and almost killed us. The worm
that is supposed to return us back
to Earth is supposed to come after

we die, not when we are giving birth
and being born. But even in the Milky
Way, we did manage to get you born;

and I will never forget the spark,
the ping of mind, the sudden gift
from nowhere that told me what I had

to do to push you out. I had
no force left in me but a voice
in my head, 'Love. Love!' A command.

The kind of love we cannot understand,
so concentrated that had it been made
of blood it would be compressed

into a pure black diamond
as large as a galaxy and as heavy
as a crushed star.

The eye would explode from looking at it.
The mouth would attach itself
like a leech and fall off, dead.

LOVE. Over and over that voice told me
what to think and do and what to use
and finally, it worked.

It cracked me open with the muscle
of a Roman god's shattering
fist and it was the god of war or the sea

called in for the emergency, on alien
wires by some Andromedan operator.
That is how you were born.

You were hardly alive, hardly you,
horribly slim-chanced. I blacked out
hard but I heard you were blue.

That voice that told me what to do
came from Andromeda. It's the only truth.
There wasn't a soul in that hospital

room told me a single thing anywhere
near as true. It was Andromedan
love that delivered you.

*

Wait till you see the doctors in Andromeda,
Cal. Yes, the doctors. It's not the afterlife,
after all, but a different life.

The doctors are whole-organism empaths,
a little like Troi on *The Next Generation*
but with gifts in all areas of the sensate self.

Not just mental or emotional empathy
but physiological. The doctors know how
you feel. They put their hands on you

and their own spleen aches, or their spirit
is tired, tendon bruised, breast malignanced,
et cetera. The patient's ills course

through the doctor's body as information,
reliable at last. There are no misdiagnoses
or cursory dismissals as if the patient

were a whiny dog who demands another
biscuit. Or shooting in the dark like good
Dr Shtep in the NICU, when you were

trying to begin living, who asked me
whether I had taken street drugs. What else
could explain your catastrophic entrance

into the human fold of the Milky Way
but the gross ignorance and disregard
of me, not her colleagues? Not even a god

we'd never share. The doctors there
are more like angels are supposed to be,
when they breathe you can sleep peacefully.

You might be surprised to hear that illness
occurs on Andromeda. That the field
of medicine is still a necessary patch of land.

Did you think I was talking you a fairy tale,
Cal? Trying to get some religious parables
into your already impassioned childhood

and indoctrinate you toward the obligations
of heaven? I am not. People still get sick
in Andromeda, and woe and death

and grief arrive each day like packets
of mail through a slot in the door.
How could it be otherwise? It is life,

after all. And despite what the religious
on Earth try to prove, no one can choose
life. We can only choose choices.

*

People get sick in Andromeda.
The difference is that people taking
care of the sick don't pretend

they know what they do not
and cannot know. In Andromeda,
everybody knows what they

need to know. Even doctors,
even patients. Even, yes, insurance
companies that don't even use

the word 'claim', certainly not in the form
of a form, in their business,
because it's just rude and heartless

to hurt further a hurt person by making
them shout in the wind, wondering
whether their pain will be approved, deemed

real, awarded validation in the form
of not bankrupting the sufferer instantly
with avalanching bills. They know that there.

We don't even need to pack our bags,
Cal. I can't be sure but how much
you want to bet they have better bags, too?

*

You'll learn to read so much more easily there,
Cal! You'll be able to see the letters
better in that atmosphere.

Maybe their alphabet has twenty-six, or maybe
thousands like Chinese characters.
It won't matter because your vision

will delineate even the finest fifteen-stroke
pictogram and you will laugh and laugh
at how the letter O looks like an open mouth

in your old language. How childish that will
seem! Your beautiful eyes may change color
with all the perfect seeing you do.

Maybe we'll miss the aqua ring around
sandy-colored irises flecked with gray and green,
little tropical islands studded

with prehistoric boulders and effusive flora,
encircled by rich, bright ocean.
Perhaps the new air in Andromeda will turn

them into brown and gray buildings,
a city in which to flick on all the lights
in a skyscraper so you can read

so far into the night I call from the next room:
'That's enough, Cal. The book will still
be there tomorrow. Time for sleep.'

*

And yes, Cal, you can roll your eyes at me,
your frumpy old mom with her wacky
ideas. I do believe in Andromeda.

You don't have to. I'll believe hard enough
for the both of us.
Because it's all my fault, you see.

I'm the one who joined that cult
of expectant mothers
who felt ourselves too delicate

and optimistic to *entertain the notion*,
as if I were inviting it to an unpleasant
afternoon tea, of something going wrong

with the birth of my child. Like so many
others, I thought it wouldn't happen
to me. In a way, it didn't happen to me.

It happened to you. And because
I wouldn't invite the terrible guests
into my psyche for goddamned tea,

I wasn't careful enough. I thought
my experience of childbirth
was a consideration. I thought

I was playing it safe by having the Best
Midwife, one who truly understood
the beauty and horror of childbirth

and who would take my side
in the ordeal (I didn't know that meant
she'd take my side *against you!*)

and who would be like a sister
to me, an expert sister and nurse and doctor
and goddess of natal wisdom

all in one, with the extra precaution
of planning to deliver in a hospital,
in case the tea-guests arrived

without an invitation. I thought the hospital
was a real hospital, too. That it knew
what it was doing and had a legal

and moral obligation to know
what it was doing. I thought that
since I was so healthy, and you were

growing so beautifully, and all the tests
and charts and balances were perfect,
that I was doing everything right.

I was arrogant. I was selfish. I wanted
to do it all correctly as if I were building
a model birdhouse at summer camp.

I was wrong. I was wrong to see the other
new mothers sighing over their sore
perinea and healthy infants

and believe that I would be like them.
Since when have I ever believed I was like
anyone else? Only when it served me,

Cal. I can blame just about anyone for what
happened to you, but ultimately it was my job
to get you into this world safely. And I failed.

There is no other way to look at it.
The other day I was walking down Court Street
in my neighborhood and saw a mother,

her child in a stroller. We were all stopped at
the same corner, waiting for the light
to change, to cross the street.

The mother was craning her neck to the left
to watch for cars, her stroller pushed out
so far ahead of her it was already

in the street, ready to go, when an unseen car
zipped fast past us, dangerously close
to her child, and the first thing the mother did

was turn to me and say, panicked,
'Did you see that? He didn't even have the light!'
But I couldn't feel any sympathy for her.

In fact, I recoiled from her safe and lucky outrage.
It's not the driver's fucking job to ensure
her child grows up safely. She could be right

and the driver wrong and her kid dead.
Two out of three is what happened instead.
She should hold him a little tighter

than usual and not waste this lesson
on being angry at a car. But I said nothing,
and, disgusted, wasted my own anger on her.

*

I supposed I could blame God. That's what cowards
do, the lazy. Like people who pretend to be
so abysmally unskilled at cooking

that someone else feeds them throughout life.
Those people are always the pickiest eaters,
have you noticed?

But let's say I won't eat potato or dairy and I can't
tolerate onion, eggs, or wheat,
what exactly would I be blaming God for?

A mistake, misjudgement, an oversight (a word
that has always amused me, its simultaneously
opposite meanings) or utter cruelty?

Weakness? Naptime? Drunk driving?
Vengefulness? Power-madness? Experimenting
with karma, playing with matches,

autopilot? Stupidity, quotas, just taking
orders? Mixing up the card files Comedy
and Tragedy? An inept assistant

who has since been fired? Poor people-skills?
Forgetfulness? Had a headache?
A cover-up? Setting things in motion so that

this poem would be written? Overworked,
underpaid? The system being broken?
Technical difficulties? Couldn't find remote?

Track-work, electrical storm, hurricane,
prayer-lines jammed by the devout,
new policies, change of direction within

the administration? On vacation, paternity
leave, sick leave, personal day, long-term
disability, short-term disability, layoffs?

Who am I to underestimate God in this way?
To imply he's some bumbling Joe,
working stiff trying to do an honest day's work?

I mean really. Who knows his workings?
If I don't know what to blame him for,
how can I blame him at all?

Perhaps there was never a flaw in the first place,
no mistakes. Perhaps God is perfect,
utterly blameless. He is what he is. Evil.

*

The gods of Andromeda, however benevolent,
cannot answer unless called.

They don't operate like Milky Way God,
who doesn't answer at all,

who is always busy offline, jetskiing
on our waterbodies, our handsqueezed

oceans of salt water, competing in dressage
though he always spooks the horses.

In those days when I would call and call
into the stupid air, if I ate something

sweet I would begin to cry, overwhelmed
by how small comfort had become.

                                                            *

So you see, Cal, we're not in particularly
good hands here. Not mine, helpless
and late, not even yours,

tiny, graceful stations the train lines
keep skipping though we've all
been waiting in the rain.

We will find our kind in Andromeda,
we will become our true selves.
I will be the mother who

never hurt you, and you will have your
childhood back in full blossom,
whole hog. We might not know

who we are at first, there, without
our terrible pain. But no flower
knows the ocean.

The sea can never find the forest,
though it can see the trees.
The succulent has no bud for salt

but one mile away the deer lick
and lick as if the sea
were in its newborn body,

replenishing the kelp of the hoof.
Though a sea would as soon
drown a deer as regenerate it,

there's a patch of mercy, sweetly
skewing between the two.
The new wind is already in us, older sister

to us all, blowing windfall and garbage
alike to those who do not deserve
either gifts or refuse.

*

And then, of course, there were the friends.
It's amazing how the ones without children
leapt to their feet in anguish

and keened, utterly genuine and broken,
made their way to our apartment with stews
and wine and tears, fruit and olive oil

and kindness so beautiful it wasn't of this world.
While our own families, our parents,
seemed so stunned (as if by a stun gun)

by their own fear that they receded
into an ether, the veiled planet Venus
for all I understood, some bright

occasional visitation and months
of silence. And, oh, the friends with precious
children. The ones who withheld,

thin-lipped. The most articulate,
sensitive souls suddenly bumbled,
tongue-tied, unable to say anything at all

but the weakest thing, the things that
actually made everything worse.
We're so scared for you. We're so sad for you.

As if our new child had died. I remembered
so vividly the ecstatic leaps of joy
I'd made without condition,

when their children were born. I knew
from several occasions that the most basic
thing to say was: *Congratulations!*

Because our beautiful baby boy
was in fact alive. I heard mostly silence
from the parents of those kids I'd celebrated.

Why on earth would it be the closest,
dearest friends to shit the most toxically
on a sad new family struggling to find

blessing where blessings were?
I wondered. It seemed to me that those
with children could ill afford

to sympathise—we were their nightmares—
how could they not be half-glad
it happened to us and not to them,

our misfortune statistically
tweaking the odds of misfortune
in their favor.

But the guilt of that relief
showed on their faces. A sight
I'll never forget.

Of course, our crisis doesn't actually
mean anything for the likelihood
of others'. It's all a trick

on the parent-heart, and we all fall for it,
how else to sleep? When I was advising
a dear student about her chances

of becoming a Rhodes scholar,
there were many grueling numbers
and pairs of numbers meant to terrify:

forty thousand applicants for twenty-four scholarships,
for example. But once she was a finalist,
I told her: your odds are now 50:50.

Not 852:1. Either you get it or you don't.
Yes, parents. I wish that my son's pain
meant your child would be spared,

but my son is not Christ. And I am no
damn Pietà Mary. In spite of our proximity,
your kid is just as likely as the next. 50:50.

By the way, the student didn't end up
a Rhodes scholar, and I told her
that, for a poet, the experience

of not winning the prize was going to be
more useful than anything else
thus far. Oh, but paltry *usefulness!*

The uses of disappointment are shit
when you just want the big damn prize
or want your child to be able to move

his limbs and talk. Back to the friends,
though, since this is the only place
I can go back to them, it seemed

to me that those most frightened
not only for their children but about
their places in the world, they were the most

grindingly inept, the least able to drum up
compassion. Those gunning for tenure
with little achievement to support it,

stay-at-home moms who had once
been talented but were now pretending
they were not in order to 'raise a family'

and to slide into inanity. I don't know what to
make of such spiritual inertia but it seems
like the same stuff racism's made of:

fear of difference. As long as it's not me,
I don't have to know anything about it.
As long as they stay the hell away from me,

it never has to be me. *As long as they stay*
weak enough they can believe they will never
be gutted by this particular pain. Not my

child, hurt like that. As long as they seem
incapable of handling such trauma,
God will never force them to.

Secret, smug believers! *God never gives you*
more than you can bear, they like to say, as if
the strong should be punished for their strength:

We can bear it. So we got it.
But what about my baby? How weak does
a newborn have to be to escape God's burdens?

And why press down so hard on Cal when
it was I who grossly claimed superhuman strength:
I know I can deliver him, I know I can

push. I don't care how much pain I'm in,
I can handle it! I can do it! I'm the strongest
fucking woman in the world!

When in fact, if I had let myself be weak,
a C-section would have kept Cal safe
and I'd never have seen the true spirit

of some of my once-close friends.
It's like that old college saying:
Alcohol kills brain cells, but only the weak ones.

I'm certain that I'm merely, unadmirably,
jealous of these friends who certainly
have their own problems,

just not the problem of an injured child,
and I have an uncomfortable,
oozing rage, as if I'd pissed myself

and had to sit in it. Rage that those
who are so fearful of my pain are the ones
who will be most spared it in their own lives.

Let them be poor, then, let them continue
their sexless marriages! Give them
a number of 'scares' after which

everything will be fine. A surgery or two.
Misery. Even give them the illnesses
and deaths of their own worthless

parents. These are the mute friends
whose children will be spared.
May they suffer every other misfortune!

I probably shouldn't be telling you
such ugly, monstrous things, Cal,
and I'm not. I'm telling the Andromedans,

to plea for a place in their galaxy.
I want to tell them *I am among weak
people here, and I am strong,*

*and I don't want to be strong anymore.
Let me be weak in your world,
among kind people who are not afraid.*

We'll just have to convince them
that we belong there, Cal, though I'm worried.
I've become bitter and angry,

not at all the kind of citizen I imagine
they'd honor with a new beginning.
But then, 'beginning' begins with 'beg'.

*

Okay, the truth?

I've been wrong or I've been lying
or I've been ignorant. It doesn't matter
which. But now it's time to give it up.

You came from Andromeda, Cal,
that other galaxy. Came to me, to us,
the moment you were born,

when the membrane between
worlds snapped and all that alien love
flooded my body. It came from you.

There was awful confusion because
you didn't seem to be of this world
and the ordinary humans

didn't know what to do. Not even me.
Mommy and her stories, those fairy
tales we have here,

wretched and unending, children
lost in the woods. No wonder you've
always looked at me so quizzically,

a story like that is too tiny to contain
Andromedan you, lost in the Milky Way,
magical boy weak from his first

intergalactic journey to my arms.
I found you, didn't I? I am here.
We found each other, we are here.

And here is where we belong, for here
is where you are you. Exactly you.
Not some other boy in some other world.

I was wrong to mourn so, *he deserves*
better and so forth. You are better.
Better than any lesser truth I could invent.

I opened my eyes from that long dream
to find you here, my perfect child.
You taught me the truth, Cal.

Accept the truth from whoever gives it,
the ancients said to your people.
The truth is that you are the truth,

a child born to a liar who is learning
to change. A dashing boy who may never
walk who traveled so far

to be here. A joyful boy who may never
talk who ruthlessly teaches
the teacher the truth

about where children really live.
Where you are alive. You are the most
perfect Calvin Makoto Teicher

of the Universe, a tough, funny
beauty of a boy who holds my hand
and blinks his eyes until I'm

excruciated, mad with love.
How hard it was for you to convince
me that I deserved that love.

My glorious son! A mother's boast
is never merely delusion. A mother
knows, if she can forgive herself

for not knowing. I know now, Cal.
Your frail arms are perfect arms.
Your uncertain eyes, perfect eyes.

Your anguish, your illness, your pain.
Your difficulty, your discovery. Your joy
is my joy and it is a perfect, boundless joy.

God must exist, a God for me after all,
and he must be good, everlastingly so,
to have given you to me.

I don't need any more proof than this.
You in my arms, your little searching fingers
on my face. Wistful, graceful

stars on a wet, clear night.
Galaxies exploding everywhere
around us, exploding in us,

Cal, faster than the lightest light,
so much faster than love,
and our Andromeda, that dream,

I can feel it living in us like *we*
are its home. Like it remembers us
from its own childhood.

Oh, maybe, Cal, we *are* home,
if God will let us live here,
with Andromeda inside us,

doesn't it seem like we belong?
Now and then, will you help me belong
here, in this place where you became

my child, and I your mother
out of some instant of mystery
of crash and matter

scattered through the cosmos,
God-scooped and poured toward
our bodies. With so much love,

somehow. I am so tired
I cannot beat my own heart anymore.
Cal, shall we stay? Oh let's stay.

We've only just arrived here,
rightly, whirling and weeping,
freely, breathing, brightly born.

So Much Synth

(2016)

I Have a Time Machine

But unfortunately it can only travel into the future
at a rate of one second per second,

which seems slow to the physicists and to the grant
committees and even to me.

But I manage to get there, time after time, to the next
moment and to the next.

Thing is, I can't turn it off. I keep zipping ahead—
well not *zipping*—And if I try

to get out of this time machine, open the latch,
I'll fall into space, unconscious,

then desiccated! And I'm pretty sure I'm afraid of that.
So I stay inside.

There's a window, though. It shows the past.
It's like a television or fish tank.

But it's ever live; it's always over. The fish swim
in backward circles.

Sometimes it's like a rearview mirror, another chance
to see what I'm leaving behind,

and sometimes like blackout, all that time
wasted sleeping.

Myself age eight, whole head burnt with embarrassment
at having lost a library book.

Myself lurking in a candled corner expecting
to be found charming.

Me holding a rose thought I want to put it down
so I can smoke.

Me exploding at my mother who explodes at me
because the explosion

of some dark star all the way back struck hard
at mother's mother's mother.

I turn away from the window, anticipating a blow.
I thought I'd find myself

an old woman by now, traveling so light in time.
But I haven't gotten far at all.

Strange not to be able to pick up the pace as I'd like;
the past is so horribly fast.

McQueen Is Dead, Long Live McQueen

There were seven colors of mourning,
one was lilac. That kind of blossom

always has its crowd, fanned out, surrounded
by crushing likeness, smell of itself.

        Fabric has to breathe,
        at least 2 percent, like skin.

        A little milkfat, elastin
        even in the gravest print.

Not knowing how to grieve can poison
like a directionless dart. And although fabric

        has been known to swirl
        and clasp, be clasped—

        without mother
        there's only art.

To hug the body: a swath, anathema,
magical, 70s lace and spacedust,

        all too far gone

to truly love. But to twist it, to learn
to hate-want. To sway, tear, burrow,

        be borrowed,
        everybody's animal.

To float like water seeking its own,
stampede like buffalo, seeking its hide.

Face painted on torso on horsehair
on chesty silk it's a deathmask

         for the stigmata slashes
         of the model's body.

           *   *

I don't think I understand what studying is.
I listen, I read, I remember, I absorb.

I let myself be moved and changed.
Is that 'studying'?

         Never five-fingered,
         you never use them all,

    gloves will be like hooves,
    split-footed hand-stitched.

When concept perceived—a womanly gist, let's say,
or a curve of mind—is more than itself (surpassing,

all maw), I make it part of me. I take it in,
drink a corrosive. I let it overtake me,

         change everything it can,
         lip to tip to rim.

My eyes just drink the fabric that covers
each surface of this world.

    Suck up the plastic
    through a polished straw.

Everything's inspiration: trees reflected
in windows on buildings, distorted buses,

endless frames, all too glass,
so much lens, textures so tall,

and once you start to see things this way,
vision's a performance, shocking

and true after all these centuries,
a Shakespearean volta, like nectar

is poison to the occasional
queen bee.

Everything actually is blurred,
not just how you see.

Glasses and shoes are solutions
to problems that are real problems,

that of blurred world,
that of touching the ground.

A glass corset for the heart
to see out its chest. For without

glasses, the eye better sees
the wind, by feeling it and closing

against its grains,
its grasses.

For without shoes, my feet become
shoes. When I am really feeling,

I get very tired, I fall asleep
for the seventeenth time

on the unfinished skirt
of glass eyes and lemon

zest hemmed first,
grown last.

I experience the world as infinite
invertedness: no wholes broken,

just potential fragments straining, skull-like,
at the seams. Anything could give.

But no, just takes
and takes and takes.

*   *

I've been trying to write the words,
'I cried. Cried really

and wetly, and for good.' Old-fashioned
writing with intense excitement:

the spell of quill
and ink spill, quelled.

What is beautiful, what is terrifying,
what is absurd in me?

Every possibility that colors
are believable, various—

not that mirage
I thought I'd seen—

and can be held apart as unreal,
too exterior, distinct from each

other wildly as sparks to seaweed
or flower to meteor.

It collapsed, can't draw it,
can't cut it out of itself.

There is no color but what's already
inside the eye, no power

or invention or new way to wake up
in the morning

        outside the seeing
        mechanism,

our own orbs. Yet I can't see myself.
I can never see you again.

I can only see from inside my skull
and when I look down

        I close everything
        not just my eyes.

I wrap my own tender nether flesh
in calfskin leather so buttery,

        melted back
        together

like so: a newborn softened
in its own mother's milk.

*   *

I awoke in a panic (no ma no ma) to the smallest day yet.
I dreamed I already

dreamed all the dreams I'd get.
This morning I dressed

in my last dress's
last dress,

fit only for a genteel gothic
murder, covered up well—airtight,

would only fit the stabbed one,
after bloodlet.

Then, like a glove.

Who wears it and where?
I will, from the bed to the chair.

Headrest, clotheshorse.
Designer and model: mutually orbiting

the best metaphor for bodiless idea.
Amorphous, amorous, amoral,

immortal. Red is dead,
said blue, to you too?

Hindquarter-gauze with silver faceclamp
and sickened ears pulled,

unskulled.

Broken backpiece. Shadow sensible
by other than sight. To smell a shadow.

To strike it. To trace it later,
to measure a body by its line.

Light's so quiet.

You'd think its cuttings, its edge-hole,
those mousy children, would squeak

at least a bit. They run like a stocking
down the leg of the mind.

Why not quieter then?

There is no body without life.
There is no mind without body.

There is no without.

Artisanal

Bring your own bread,
your breath, your own
mouth, open

all night. What wouldn't
I give to fill it?
I can't see

my breath yet catch it
again and again
like a magic coin

I use to buy myself
back from the self–
chamberbox,

that dank fromagerie,
again and again.
In its dark robe

worn open, the night—
blind prince
of the black cat—

has a page for us all.
What wouldn't I give
to fill it?

Such is the dreary
unwritten history
of hunger,

of what to say to stay
alive. We don't
write it down.

We can't keep it down.
Why bring it up?
Burn it all down.

Make it new. A real
writer makes do.
Famous last words.

Not even ink makes
the best ink; wine
better spreads a stain

and the mouth is
already wet—the better
to contain a fire

or catch a fish
or tell a story sharpening
the point of the last

meal—that incredible
question, star of dread.
My own words,

eaten like a cheese
requested for the death
of it, ending my sentence,

and the one after it.
There's always one after it.

Wound

As if to woo
not to wow.

I didn't dazzle like I expected
to. My body,

interracial & grumous,
either overly looked at

or totally overlooked.
My whole body isn't anything,

just a collection. What is
truly midmost me

is injury, an old one,
decrepit unreal thread opening

new self-holes, new tears
pronounced like *air*

not *fear*. The tear knits
back together,

stitches melt to keep
the wound soft, keep

a space which fills and fills
but never fills.

Disappointment's all right
& emptiness

can pulse weird useful energy.
But I'm most afraid

of panicked mind alone,
silent, in the end.

When fear becomes
an ability to split myself off

and my body is just another
kind of sourdough

hardening in the window
of the failing bakery.

Not even children stop
to look. They don't

want anything anymore,
hungry or not.

They too have had enough
of taking to fear

what gives of itself
without and to no end.

Dress Form

Myself I'm like a dress my mother made
me, a fabric self split open with a sigh
as I grew and—bewildered or proud

or full of rage—patched with nicer
material than we'd had before. I got
the sense it was all wasted on me.

But a needle's sharp to pierce, is itself
pierced—so as to sew like I was taught.
Like I learned: no dress could ever be

beautiful or best if it had me in it.
I was the stain in a place we couldn't fix.
Having fallen on a slicer of some kind.

Double-seamed, scabbed over, a new body
pocket in the pattern. How to stitch up
that wound right into the clean vertical rip

in some on-sale flannelette?
I'd never again be so cold. Skin's holey not holy.
In mad winter alone with drink, I think:

tattoo needles don't use thread but ink
to mark a place in this ever-moving skin
and that wound is ornament. But who

needs a mark to know what's marked?
I would pray to the dark in the dark.
But what did I ask for, what did I know

to ask for? Nonfatal wounds: they're there
when we die, deliquescent, vibrating like a drum
skin just after each beat moves off.

A part of music. A way a body keeps time,
is time's keeper, vigilant till time up and goes
to find another body. Another's warmth

and shelter. Or related injuries. Anyone
who hurts another was hurt that same way,
so how far back behind our backs do we go

to finally find the first hurt; whose finger
points to say, 'You! You're the one who god
knows why started a cycle of unending pain,'

to someone's child in short pants?
A baby just torn a hole in her amnion swirl?
And what of me? I can't tell where my flesh

meets there rest of me, ragbag full of rags,
shot full of holes but that's just the way cotton
and silk and everything I said up till now looks

when it hits the air and is cried on. I'm so inside
out I evaporated entirely already as August does,
my actual dress shredded at the seams—

unsalvageable. Who would ever love me like this?
And just like that, I stopped thinking about it.
I agree to meet you at the ferry heading to a place

neither of us wants to go but both just said
sure, I'll go… if you want! We should turn back,
nobody said. Oh we should before it's too late,

nobody said again, insistent this time.

But I'm the Only One

who'll walk across a fire for you,
growled Melissa. That song
blared out from all four of
our bedrooms' tape decks,
often simultaneously, as if
that song were the only one
we all loved, the only one we
could agree on that summer
in the dyke loft, just when it
all started to change. Catherine
was moving out, to SoHo to
live with Melanie. So Shigi's
girlfriend DM took her room.
But not for long; they broke up
and Michelle moved in, shortly
after Cynthia came. *Tonight you
told me that you ache for something
new.* This was way before we'd
even dreamed we'd have to rent
out Shigi's office to Erin as a fifth
bedroom. Without Catherine we
couldn't afford the loft, but we
didn't know that yet. At the time
we thought everyone was poor
like us—we weren't the only ones.
We all smoked constantly, anyone
could afford to smoke back then.
Catherine bummed my last butt
but I know I saw her new carton
in the freezer. She didn't want
to open it yet, was trying to
cut back. This was before we
almost got the gas cut off, before
we lost electricity the first of
many times. After Justine had

been bullied out with her three
cats but Kristen—whom we
suspected was asexual and not
really lesbian—was still hanging
on even though she adopted yet
another cat into the loft without
asking. It was only one more,
she reasoned, but we already
had Seether, Amber, Balzac,
Gigli, and now Eva Luna.
Anna and Jackie came by,
they were friendly to me, but
Tjet and Julie weren't. T and J
were Clit Club. A and J were
literary. Then Michelle and
Shigi secretly slept together,
a disaster, and Cynthia got
kicked out for being bi and
then bringing a guy to the loft,
but that summer, before all that,
just after I'd been dumped by
the girl I'd moved to NYC
to be with, and just after I'd
invited my first college girl-
friend to come visit me
(not sure what I expected,
but she was the only one
who was willing to fly out)
but before I met Natira.
Our month-long affair
wasn't great but still pretty
damn good, she was the only
one I'd liked in a long time. I
hadn't met Sayeeda yet, at
Jackie's book party—Jackie
and Anna I think were broken
up by then. After Stefanie
but long before Tina, before

Jamie had even met Tina,
this song played everywhere,
every day, ceaselessly, so it
started to seem that we were
Melissa—that Cassandra—
foretelling in a ragged voice:
'And I'm the only one who'll
drown in my desire for you.'
We meant that we too were
willing to do anything to
prove we were the only one
for someone that one summer.

A Mix Tape: 'Don't You (Forget About Me)'

> Think of the tender things that we were working on.
>
> SIMPLE MINDS

Such a delicious pain in the ass to make,
on a double deck if you were lucky,

otherwise you had to drop the needle
onto the precise groove as your left

index hit PLAY/RECORD, taking all
afternoon or many. Mistakes, thinking

too hard about what you wanted
to tell the person but couldn't say

any other way. It was always
'I love you,' didn't you know?

Mix tape: private language, lost art,
first book, cri de coeur, X-ray, diary.

An exquisitely direct and sweet
misunderstanding. We weren't

fluent yet but we lived in its nation,
tense and sweaty for an anthem.

Receiving a mix tape could be major,
depending on from whom; giving one

to someone in public was a dilemma.
You had to practice. Would you say,

nonchalantly, 'Oh, here, I made you
a mix tape?' By the lockers? In class?

Ugh! But giving it over in private
could be worse, especially arranging it.

You never picked the best song off
the album, definitely not the hit single.

The deeper the cut the deeper buried
your feelings for that person. You didn't

know? Not all lovesongs, though—
that would make you seem obsessed,

boring. They should know you're fun
and also funny and dark-hearted

and, importantly, unpredictable.
A 'Blasphemous Rumours' for every

'Only You.' And sexy! Though not
Prince's moaners—not 'Erotic City,'

not 'Darling Nikki'! But what?
Not Top 40 stylish, with a sly angle,

'70s funk, some Stevie Wonder, like you've
got background you don't really have.

As it records, you have to listen to each
song in its entirety, and in this way

you hear your favorite song with the ears
of your intended, as they hear it, new.

This was the best feeling of your young
life. Then the cold chill of suddenly hearing

in your third-favorite INXS song a lyric
you'd break out in hives over if you thought

they thought you thought that about them
when they heard it (*there's something*

about you, girl, that makes me sweat).
The only thing worse was the tape

running out a full minute before the end
of 'There Is a Light That Never Goes Out'.

You never got it right, not even once.
That was part of the mix tape's charm,

to your dismay. Did it ever win you
love? You never fell for anyone

else's mix either. Sometimes cool,
mostly was just someone else's

music in a case dense with tiny
handwriting to get all those titles in.

So much desire in those squeezed-in
letters. Not 'Love me!' so much as

'Listen to me! Listen to me always!'
So that's really it, right? Maybe

you thought someday you'd make
a mix tape that your splendid friend,

your lucky star, your seventh stranger,
would take a pen to, punching in

the little plastic tabs which meant,
as you well know, it could never be

taped over again. They'd never use
your mix tape to make another mix tape

to give away, or to copy a friend's album
they didn't like enough to buy, joining all

the okay tapes in caddies stacked up a wall
or thrown in the backseat of the Datsun,

then in moving boxes, stored in parents'
garages, five for a buck at a yard sale,

buried in a landfill, or, saddest of all,
discarded on the street, purple script

still aswirl on the white label FOR YOU—
JUST BCUZ. Shiny brown ribbon

tangled, strangled, never again to play
out what had to be said just that way.

A Mix Tape: The Hit Singularities

(SIDE A)

1 *'Like a Virgin'*—MADONNA

How to look out the window
and see something other

than the sea of purple apricot
that velvet sunset left

on my terrifying private sky,
in 1983?

2 *'Cruel Summer'*—BANANARAMA

They didn't last the afternoon,
any of those three dates in a week,
three new guys I'd met.

I said yes to a drive to the beach,
a lunch at Sizzler and lunch
at a salad place.

I thought I was getting ready,
Sun In in my perm, but we could tell
by the silence.

It wasn't hungry or angry. Didn't
want a stronger stranger,
or even dessert.

Just caressed everything hopeless
with no muscles at all. Thanks!
See you in school.

3 *'Let's Go Crazy'*—PRINCE

Tonight's hemophiliac moon
(talented cheat) is brilliant

in the role of understudy
to the sometimes mad eye of Venus.

Or:

Being a smart girl who wants
to be in love is like breaking a leg

in a boring accident (sidewalk trip)
but the wound gets a disease (gangrene)

so everyone looks at you funny
but they don't really notice you.

4 *'Nobody's Diary'*—YAZ

How do I deceive myself?
Do I act my happiness?

Am I good at acting it?
I live in a large box of air

playing records so unhappily.
I can't forget how you looked

at me, like I wasn't me and you
weren't you. How to change?

How to change everything
into everything you like?

5 *'How Soon is Now'*—THE SMITHS

Blood in the mouth
is so familiar, metal

in liquid form come
up to nourish source.

So we put to lips what
cuts us: paper, wood,

wire, knife, teeth.
I bite my tongue in two

when I smell your hair,
that Aqua Net. When

will I know the smallest
hair? The softer things?

6 *'You Spin Me Round (Like a Record)'*—DEAD OR ALIVE

Words: the berries of the cosmos,
plucked from their system,

then changed beyond belief
because you don't believe me.

(SIDE B)

1 *'Do You Really Want to Hurt Me?'*—CULTURE CLUB

Against ourselves
we stand no chance—
we chop our wood,
jack our trades, gas
our cars, shave our heads
bare in solidarity with
not dying. We are
the miracle meat.
Sandwiches nobody
buys, wrapped in plastic
on display against
our wishes against
ourselves again.

2 *'I Ran (So Far Away)'*—A FLOCK OF SEAGULLS

I ran away only to prove
I chose my next move somehow.

Really you did not lose me:
you walked away. I saw there waiting

but you were gone. Only then did I run,
to salvage a mile or two of my own.

I don't know how much of my own story
is true and what I've had to believe.

Really I think I just sat there self-thinking
the same cruel sentences:

You fool yourself, you do. And you know it, liar.
I couldn't get away.

3 *'Here Comes the Rain Again'*—EURYTHMICS

No kind Nana
with papery hands to click
her knitting needles

and tell you that memory
itself used to have memory.
This wet dump doesn't

remember falling year
after year, but it did, does,
the very same stuff.

Water is One, to Old Earth-
Sky, even if we divide it
by tasks, titles, time.

4 *'Words'*—MISSING PERSONS

      Do you hear me? Do you care?

If words were material
and not ether, ink, rivulet
of breath in space,

they'd have a hand-stitched
quality, each a starsplat
of sleep on a plain white

tight cotton sheet that robots
wove on their industrial looms.
They want us comfortable.

5 *'New Moon on Monday'*—DURAN DURAN

Changeling starlings landing
on a line of verse or vine of voice

so singular

it's not inhuman but unihuman.
Simon says he's synced

to a perfect keyboard,
there's truth in synth.

That's what synth means:
to make true. An everglow

lost among the speechless.
Le bon mot swallows the night.

6 *'(Keep Feeling) Fascination'*—THE HUMAN LEAGUE

I'm blinded by vision, like an artist
who paints miniature landscapes
and portraits on a grain of sand
using a microscope and tweezers,

who yells 'Fuck!' when the tiny
brush with its single mousehair slips
and ruins the mountaintop the artist
has been scaling all morning, hoping

to peak by lunch. It was never going
to be a masterpiece, we know that,
but it does hold fast whatever art is in us,
that thing that blooms like failure and is.

Is There Something I Should Know?

I know you're watching me every minute of the day yeah.
I've seen the signs and the looks and the pictures.
They give your game away yeah.

There's a dream that strings the road
With broken glass for us to hold,
And I cut so far before I had to say:
Please please tell me now!

DURAN DURAN

If I were fourteen again, I wouldn't be in this situation now,
trying to write without a pen. Isn't blood a woman's ink?

Back then, whatever I scratched into my well-filled,
ill-hid diary was my existence, and those scribblings—

fast as I could think, or slow as if carving out a spell—
formed the outer periphery of me, the inner lining.

The rest of me: juice, some sponge,
electricity like synth riffs not interested in bringing light.

Sometimes I just dumped rage and hurt, yearning
for finer feelings, not the indignities I suffered.

But if I suffered sharply, I could scarcely trace it soft:
'You think you're pretty, dork?' spat at me at school

transcribed as: 'Swirling Ugly Vortex. Stupid Me!'
alone in my room later. I scrounged for the words,

keeping the scope of it all very open, universal,
somehow dramatising *and* minimising.

'The worst thing in the world
is that nobody cares, not even me!!!'

Who was I kidding? Even in my private diary
I performed myself to an audience of one, no one.

A stock character playing to an empty house,
though I'd no theater experience at all.

I lied outright, wrote daydreams as if true,
was all-knowing and exquisite, simultaneously

the worst person ever to have lived. Adolescence
is all absolutes: if bad, one must be the very worst

to avoid being mistaken for average.
To be ordinary was just being invisible,

and surely slow naked death by ants hurts less than that.
The middle always was for losers. The middle seat,

the middle-aged, the middle child, the middle finger,
middle school, middling.

I remember writing: 'One thing I know
I definitely am not is: a totally bizarre person.'

Only a few years later my entire persona
craved a real and lasting bizarreness, I fashioned

it out of my relentless wholesomeness,
easily, actually, because hallucinogens are great

for making you think you actually are weird.
But that came later. In junior high I was a kid

under the impression I was supposed to act
grown up, and that meant knowing who I was

and how groups started or shaped, like on the bus
or at the lockers if you didn't go to the same grade school

as a lot of people who all knew each other, and what
to wear and how my own body worked at least.

At least how to become friends with people
I liked without just mimicking them and trying

to figure out how to join their group? But how?
And boys could tease you or tell you anything, do

anything. How'd you know where you stood?
Every scene—lunch, P.E., English—had different rules,

invisible: they changed depending on who had power.
That was never you. You couldn't just be yourself anywhere.

There was an amazing story in me, one that I would live
powerfully, in wet velvet poetry: *And you wanted*

to dance so I asked you to dance, but fear is in your soul...
the voice of Simon Le Bon permeated all those

new cells, the bloody ones, the ripenings, and I knew
his love was deep. Too deep, maybe, hard to know what

anything he sang meant. He was also a little whiny.
The perfect pretty pout of John Taylor, however,

with that sunken chest—fetishised forever after that—
was the New Romantic, graceful, not quite as lurid

with makeup as Nick Rhodes but still breathtaking
in girlish man-ness. Perfect perfect,

all absorbed in brooding sounds and slow,
distant love that maybe insinuated sex

but was more like helpless desire, a beautiful
man mooning over...me? Much emotional

clutching of said sunken treasure before
glamorously running down the wet

tarmac in a flapping linen suit to catch a plane
to the next *some people call it a one-night stand*

but we can call it paradise. Yes, I'd be left, newly
a woman, languid and a little tearful thinking

about my erotic awakening in the bungalow
by really any of Duran Duran except Andy.

*   *

Before pubescence's acrid synthesis—those 700 days—
I was a kid: all glossy grubby greatness, jumping through

sprinklers, full-tilt rollerskating, running down
the street while running my mouth, just as often

riveted to the silent endlessness
demanded by a beautiful or terrifying story: I'd hide

and lose and seek and find myself in every page:
laughing, rereading and then re-rereading

out loud, disbelieving the details till my system
could absorb them like the nutrients they were.

Sara Crewe was so kind I'd disappear into her
and only a perfect girl remained.

Surely I'd have adored her in silks or in rags.
How I yearned to show her that I, too, knew

that being good meant to *love goodness* and
not just act nice to get what I wanted.

In *Maggie Adams, Dancer*, I'd be Joyce—sure, okay.
I didn't mind! The slightly chunky ballerina

ever-cast as the gingerbread lady or Rat King,
never Sugar Plum. I would tend the sad traumas

of Maggie, slender and spotless, just trying her best
against that evil wall of perfection

she kept slamming her lithe body against.
Maggie's problems didn't make you pity her,

unlike Lupe the religious Latina who was anorexic
and died! Or Joyce, who predictably tanked because

of her wrong body type. She was only fooling
herself. Maggie had snags that made you admire her.

The kind of protagonist whose beauty and high-spirited
intelligence are cast as flaws: she hates her gorgeous,

'unruly' red corkscrew curls and her 'too long' legs,
her mortifying but adorable blushing, a temper

that flares at unfairness, her embarrassing way
of always blurting out helpful truths that move

the plot along, deepening and developing
all the supporting characters.

By the end of Maggie Adams, my 700 days were well
underway. My love for Maggie changed

and was now, I suspected, unwholesome. God would
have frowned, or so the dogma went then.

Sure it seemed okay to *think* any old thoughts,
especially if you didn't say anything, but the problem

with God is that he was supposedly there in your
thoughts already, could hear them. So why pray?

I wondered. If he can already hear me, aren't all
my thoughts, then, even the sexy ones, prayer?

And how could he understand what I was thinking
about Maggie if he hadn't read the book?

Whoever heard of God reading? Like curled
up on the sectional reading about teen ballerinas

or snooping in a twelve-year-old's diary?
Anything that happened between those covers,

on those sheets of paper, was safe, and my thoughts
were protected from God's snooping.

It wasn't just Maggie, not only kind and beautiful
white girls—though that's who I usually fell for,

and underdogs, too. I could love so variously
so many kinds of people in books,

not just the victim in *Blubber* but her tormentors,
the ignored twin Wheeze, the boy in the peach,

the boy who masturbated, strong weird Anastasia,
Casey Child of the Owl, Deenie with scoliosis,

the girl with anorexia, the girl who was raped,
the girl who didn't speak, the girl who died.

Heathcliff and Cathy, both, of course, though
Cathy less. She didn't deserve Original Goth Guy

and was a goody-goody. I hoped one day I'd see
someone in real life and have that 'love'-like feeling

152

(*I try to discover a little something to make me sweeter*),
whisper, 'It's happened!' and touch myself in awe:

'This is the me it happened to!'
(*Oh baby refrain from breaking my heart!*)

Me, once sick or strange or poor or unlucky,
somehow now utterly loved, absolutely chosen,

lifted out of dreary life in our subdivision,
sleeping well though the occasional engine

revving out of control down our through-road.
During the 700 days I began to understand

that when love happened, I'd become real.
(*I'm so in love with you, I'll be forever blue.*)

I wouldn't be living as one of 'us'. Part of an old family.
This sad unit started by them, my parents,

which had zero logic and seemed to have nothing
to do with me. (*That you give me no reason*

why you're making work so hard!) Sometimes what's good
for everyone forced each individual to act

compensatorily (*that you give me no*),
nobody getting what they wanted (*that you give me no*).

I wanted to yell, jump, skate, sing, write, rant!
I wanted to be loved, to love, to find gentleness

and sexy strength and not be stuck being me
(*Soul, I hear you calling*),

to somehow lift the ME up into some other world
where someone (who? this was the great mystery)

might lose himself (herself?) in me (*Oh baby please!*),
the heroine of this most wonderful story.

Such a satisfying story that I wouldn't have to diet
or worry about my clothes or how awkward my jokes were

(*that you give me no*). My quotations were always in character,
endearing, and if I was weird, that was part

of what made me so much fun to read, 'quirky' (*that you
give me no*), my unpredictability and sweetness and nuzzly,

irrepressible oddness and charisma. My inelegance
transformed into a set of classic and eternal qualities

propelling the story to greatness. (*Give a little respect. To. Me!*)
Without that story, I just said stupid things

that killed me late at night, squirming at the memory
of my idiocy. I told Jenny her hair was like straw?

I knew she was mean but I thought she was stupid
enough to take it as a compliment. But she detected

the intended insult and hissed at me.
Now she knows how I really feel about her,

and I'm just as mean as her, but obviously dumber.
(*Give a little respect! To! ME!*)

This feeling of being out of control of what I said
was happening more frequently.

I used to be able to say exactly what I wanted,
often disastrously ('I don't want to leave the mall,'

for example, I said once when I was seven-ish.
I must have been really bad, impossible,

because my mom drove away and left me there
outside wandering the concrete planters.

I was scared. She didn't come back for a long time.
I pretended to be interested in the shrubbery,

acting like I didn't care, especially when I saw her
car pull up. I got in, hoping I seemed indifferent.

I didn't want her to know I was scared. Was I?
Why did I want to stay at the mall anyway?)

'I want to see a movie with Lisa H.! Her mom's driving!'
'I don't want to go to Japanese school!'

'I hate piano lessons!' and overruled again
and again until finally I wasn't. And decades later

I mourn the unlearned Japanese language and the piano.
What did I know about what I wanted?

What I said I wanted was ignored, until finally
a parent got fed up with hearing me whine

and then it was, 'Fine! You don't want to go,
you don't have to go. Your grandmother wanted

you to learn piano, but fine! You win.'
That it was Nana who wanted us to learn piano

seemed to confirm how pointless that would be.
When we saw her once or twice a year, she'd

again say that once we learned to play the piano,
we'd be the 'belles of the ball'!

But I was into Duran Duran and Madonna and Prince.
Not to mention Dead or Alive and Yaz and Erasure.

I was into the future. So much synth. So much
silvery, zingy computer music: *I wouldn't say that*

you were ruthless or right. I couldn't see from so far.
Oh god, is there any music as good as what you heard

at fourteen? It never occurred to me that the music
forever imprinted on Nana's young psyche

was the piano, played by a girl luckier and richer than she.
The one girl loved enough to be given lessons

was the source of teen joy and envy in her group,
and she wished this glory for us. Of course it didn't occur

to me. (How could Nana have been a teenager?)
I was accustomed to being ignored (unfairly, I thought)

and then listened to (but what did I know?)
at the wrong times, almost, it seemed, at precisely

the wrong times, like how I always choose the polar
opposite direction of where I am supposed to go,

if I am going by instinct. (*Was I chasing after rainbows?*
One thing for sure you never answered when I ca-a-alled.)

Or how it feels when forced to call a side of a coin:
heads is the winner's call but it loses as often as tails,

while tails is the countermove which should have
some advantage but doesn't. When you get your call

it feels just like luck, but when you don't it's failure.
This is the feeling of having duped yourself into thinking

you had some control over that awful double-edged
mystery we call 'chance'. Randomness or opportunity.

Both were terrifying. *But I still can feel those splinters of ice.*
I look through the eyes of a stranger.

I remember convincing myself, when I was thirteen,
that I hadn't 'really' gotten my period. This was because

I'd only gotten it once, then twice, then three times,
and it seemed unreal it'd be here to stay.

My first menstruation (which was never what we called it
even once) came a month before I turned thirteen, and it felt

too fast to be twelve with it. I knew I wasn't 'a woman'
but a big kid still not allowed to say bad words,

yet was suddenly supposed to be fluent in a rough
and dirty language now that I had 'the curse'

and was 'on the rag'. Even if we said it cute ('riding
the little white surfboard'), I thought it was gross

to get it at twelve. Where did I get that idea?
I knew from *Are You There God? It's Me, Margaret*

that you were supposed to pray, hope, and wait for it,
celebrate it, tell everyone in your family.

I thought mine was too brown, poop-like, hardly a
glamorous womanly thing I'd read about in a great book!

It didn't seem ladylike or sexy at all. It was just scary
and messy and had to be hidden from everyone

because everyone knew it was totally disgusting.
If you ever got your period at school in such a way

that anyone knew, you'd never get over the humiliation.
You'd have to convince your parents to move.

This scenario terrorised us. No way was I ready
to handle such a delicate social secret.

Whether anyone else was, who knew?
We couldn't talk about it because some people

hadn't gotten it yet and were shy about that, others shy
because they did and didn't want anyone to know.

You weren't supposed to ask. *For rumors in the wake*
of such a lonely crowd, trading in my shelter for danger.

Every month it felt like some sordid and revolting thing
was happening to me, and it was.

No one discussed it or acknowledged it
even though we ALL READ THE JUDY BLUME.

Basically, all the stories I'd read or heard about
what it was really like to become a woman

made me rather expect a kind of slow, gorgeous
liquefaction after which I'd emerge a cross

between Jessica Rabbit and Denise Huxtable
except that I was half-Japanese, and so neither fit,

but nothing fit anyway. Not Dorothy Gale or Coco
from *Fame* or Strawberry Shortcake

(*I'm changing my name just as the sun goes down,*
walking away like a stranger) or Cyndi Lauper

or Punky Brewster or Smurfette or Madonna
or, well that's it. Who else was there to shadow?

(...*such a lonely crowd*) Cartoon, fashion plate,
tragedy, infantile aesthete, video clown, sex paradox.

Dimensions of two, not three.
Never four. Oh how time traveled through a mind

and body shifting from Anne of Green Gables
to Samantha Fox in 700 days.

For the better part of a year, I kept my arms crossed
in front of my chest as if in a bad mood,

hoping no one would see how my swollen mushroom
nipples poked out my shirt. I was afraid

of a bra, convinced that everyone would see
my straps and know that I was aware I had breasts

and that I knew what it was like to have them,
to 'shoulder' that responsibility, understand all

the jokes that went along with them. Imperative to hide
your period; impossible to hide your breasts.

My mom begged me to wear my 32AA to school,
but I wore three shirts instead. It was like falling off a cliff

in the dark. I hit the ground in seventh grade,
at a new school where all the eighth graders wore bras,

where suddenly lack of bra straps would be
the source of embarrassment. Poor Shannon,

my best friend who was still flat: six months ago
I'd prayed to be like her, and now I felt sorry for her.

She looked so short and skinny and small,
like a fourth grader! But I had other worries:

the dark hair on my lower legs nobody else
seemed to have, and which my short sweatsocks

didn't cover during drill team/gym,
though I pulled them up as high as I could.

Pure misery, those tiny blue shorts—
but not that tiny, I had to get the Mediums,

which made me feel fat when another Shannon
and a Lori got Extra Extra-Small, but okay when

a Tahnya and a Kathleen got Extra Extra-Large.
How could my size, exactly in the middle,

make it seem I was both extremes?
In middle school, running in the middle of the pack

in the middle of the road, now offered precious
invisibility that wasn't as safe as it seemed.

You could easily become nobody.
And why was there no such size as Extra Medium?

Nobody showered, because people would see you
naked. Some Ramona wasn't even wearing a bra

at this point, just a little girl's undershirt with a bow.
We weren't mean. We didn't have to be.

She curled over in self-loathing, yanking her sweater
on, her jeans, face a tomato hurled at herself.

Oh god seventh grade! Just staring at my pale leg
and my dark hairs. I knew my mom wouldn't let me shave,

just like she wouldn't let me use tampons, only pads.
Not that I asked. I was too embarrassed to ask:

she just bought pads for me, a new box in my underwear
drawer every month, while there was always a box of Playtex

plastic tampons on the toilet tank in her bathroom.
I tried one, stuck it up there and couldn't feel a thing.

Amazing! But I was so confused to see blood running
down my leg. So I read the directions. Ohhhh!

You stick the tampon in, holding on to just one tube, push
the bottom tube into the first, and pull BOTH plastic parts out

and put them in the trash! You inject yourself with the tampon!
OHHH! You really did have to read the directions.

I was never going to figure that out myself.
Anyway, tampons were way better because you

couldn't see them and they didn't slip, but you also
didn't know whether they were full or not. So?????????????

Accidents no matter what. After stealing enough mom-pons,
my mom finally bought me my own Slender Regulars,

which I knew from magazines were for teens.
Those teens looked so glossy, their fluids regulated;

they rode on sparkling streams of lovely teenage cuteness.
Their periods undetectable, their gym shorts Extra Small,

their legs either hairless by nature
or by their mom's permission, their skin flawless

and their head-hair flowing. I stared at them in magazines;
the ones I got were *Young Miss* and *Seventeen.*

Their fluidity seemed to carry them straight to stardom,
adored by all. My chunky fluids got on my sheets.

My greasy bangs covering my eyes, I stared at myself
in the mirror: *What kind of butt is that? It doesn't seem…right.*

161

I don't know how I convinced my mom to let me
shave my legs. I only remember that the problem

disappeared, so she must have let me. At some point,
my younger sister stole a razor, my mom's or mine,

I'm not sure, and sliced up her shin in the bath.
Long strips of skin lay in the tub after

our parents took her to the hospital.
It looked worse than it was (the inverse of the usual),

and I recall them looking like beige carrot peels
turning brown. She'd felt the same desperation I did.

It hadn't occurred to me anyone but me could have it.
The thing is: no one looked us in the eye and told us

anything (*Please please tell me now!*), and maybe
we wouldn't have listened (*Is there something I should know?*)

and maybe reading about puberty in pamphlets
was somewhat effective since we were such good readers,

but pamphlets either gave numbered instructions:
   (1) Read instructions before use.
   (2) Raise one foot up on the toilet as illustrated
or talked in euphemisms: 'feeling like a lady

during your special time!' one said. Another: 'Pretty is
as pretty does!' Pretty does what? I thought.

Pretty IS what? What could that possibly mean?
If even the grown-ups were too embarrassed to talk

to us about blood and mess and cramps and hormones,
it must be really bad. As bad as divorce or cancer—

that level of hush, with whispers around the people
involved. Our bodies' changes were kept secret

from us alone; everyone else could see. (*People stare and
cross the road from me.*) But I had my secrets, too.

Wanted to be wanted by someone I wanted.
(*Do you feel the same 'cuz you don't let it show*)

How complicated that desire turned out to be, now,
with this weird new thing: being wanted by those

I didn't want at all, or at least I didn't think so,
but how to know how to know who you want?

Aside from knowing for sure that if John Taylor
could carry you off with those skinny arms of his

you'd totally do it, who in real life was there to like?
You might get laughed at no matter who you picked,

unless he picked you. But that's not you wanting
who you want, right? And by 'wanting' what

do you mean? You're a good girl, you have to be nice—
if you're not, the consequences are not so nice:

you've seen a loudmouthed girl elbowed in the tits
by a boy in a laughing group. She got quieter, 'nicer'—

so even when someone's totally off-the-charts rude,
lewd, or crude, the only known response is a polite one.

The rude ones count on this, of course.
Ancient ploy: convince young girls they lack

some undisclosed quality of such importance
it's the only thing men and boys will ever want

them for, to persuade them they're so defective
they're lucky he's a cool guy who accepts all

the flaws no one else would put up with, a nice
guy who wants to help them feel beautiful

by inserting his penis, often without warning,
into their precious young bodies and use them,

their whole dear romantic trusting selves,
to get his pleasure from their orifice, which

is what he spent all that energy trying to procure,
even though he claimed he had better

things to do. He thinks he's a cool customer
in an antiques store who sees a priceless treasure

and knows he can convince the seller it's a piece
of junk, dented and dirty, she's lucky to get five

bucks for it. He's the only one who understands
this to be a deal, a sale, a score.

A fourteen-year-old girl doesn't have any idea how rare
her own body is. She's only ever lingered over its flaws,

ever since childhood ended,
around 524 days ago, eternity in reverse.

She thinks it is worth nothing; she's not a place
where treasures can be bought cheap or stolen.

She thinks it's kind of sweet that someone noticed
her, that maybe it's a sign she's lovable after all.

Because he's convinced her that his desire is hers,
and that being 'fuckable' is a compliment.

What I learned at fourteen was that there was never a short
supply of boys twelve years old, men of seventy,

every age in between, who were interested and willing
and didn't even need to be asked to give an opinion

on my fuckability. And no matter what I thought of *them*,
it was *their* opinion that would never be omitted

in the final tally of my total worth.
And that nowhere in the world would my opinion

on *their* fuckability (what a joke!) ever be considered
relevant in any circumstance or for any reason.

I knew that men could walk past me and call me 'slut'
and 'nice-tits' and 'oriental pussy' and I couldn't even

complain about it because it was embarrassing,
and furthermore, bragging!

Yes! If you told anyone, that person gave you a weird,
pinched look as if you'd just given yourself

this lewd compliment and were fishing for more.
If you told anyone that some fifty-year-old man

waggled his tongue at you out his car window
then stuck his index finger through a hole he'd made

with his other hand ('Then how was he steering?'
someone was sure to ask with a doubling smirk),

driving slow past you as you walked on the highway
to the mall, you were surely making it up.

And it just made you look bad if you said it,
as if saying it was what made it really happen.

If you told anyone your own age that a big, tall guy
a little older than you whispered, 'I bet you're slutty,'

your friends would ask how he even knew you (ha ha!)
so well. (You're a virgin, haven't even kissed.)

Because the only person you could tell was another
girl like you, who was so confused about what it all meant

that we figured it must have meant nothing, since
nothing was done about it and nothing about it mattered.

If you told your mom, you wouldn't
be able to go anywhere or wear anything halfway cool.

No peach lipgloss. No two-inch Cherokee sandals, on which I
learned to balance the height of a heel and the price of the pair

with social correctness and mom's all-important okay.
Because she was buying. And she was short so she was okay

generally with a little heel height even if you were fourteen.
But if you told your mom, you'd be in Mary Janes

and so would your twelve-year-old sister. If you told your dad,
well, this was unthinkable. You could never tell your dad.

Telling your dad meant you were failing.
A baby bird crushed underfoot after that first

unsuccessful leap from the nest. Maybe it meant
something was wrong with the nest or the branch

was too high, but no one ever thought that.
You were just a loser.

It hurt when a man yelled out of a car but there was no
way to feel it. There was no synapse connecting

wound to brain, no way to know where it hurt or why.
It was inward, and if no one noticed, it just as well

didn't happen. The wound was never compared
to what might have blossomed there in a world where men

did not throw cruel, vicious 'compliments' at young girls;
the wound was only ever compared to the worst-

case scenario: the car stopping, the duct tape and the trunk.
You didn't even have to say the word *rape*. It was

assumed that's what the crime would be. What other
imaginable thing could an unknown man in a car want with you?

Your money? Your extorted promise to renew
the municipal contract for the mob's energy company?

Revenge for turning down his nephew for prom date?
Just looking for someone to talk to?

There's nothing else a fourteen-year-old has that anyone would
want enough to commit a crime for. So you should be happy

you just got yelled at. You should feel relieved and lucky
and happy that the only thing that you are valued for

was not taken by force and was instead merely jeered at
and threatened. When you learn that you are supposed

to feel lucky and happy because you weren't raped and killed,
you are already, in this, being brutally hurt

in a central, deep, and formative place. This is never admitted.
This is never permitted acknowledgement.

If you say this, someone will refute it. So I will say it here.
We can't know the extent of the damage caused

by the constant threat of rape: the mutations, the atrophy,
emptiness, self-mutilation, isolation, fear, flying fucks,

can seem defensive, bitchy, *loca*, now you are too damaged
to have any say-so. So no wonder bad things happen.

Everything you say is crazy. Even if nothing bad ever happens
to you, whatever you could have been if not for this damage

isn't real or considered valuable, so losing it is not a loss.
You never mattered. Not your safety today or your potential.

It never matters that every experience you'll ever have
will be curtailed, limited, cut, and that you will participate

in that with every sentence you speak ending in a question
so as not to anger anyone who needs to be right?

You know that being right isn't worth being assaulted and killed?
You learned it young? Maybe it kept you alive?

When you are fourteen and trying to become yourself
and you learn this self is quickly becoming a target

but you can't tell anyone, you dodge and go fast, get it over with,
you hurt yourself first so no one can do it to you; you choose

to give your virginity to the first person who seems to be
the kind of person who wouldn't take it

in a mean way. You don't know if you felt anything.
You don't know if you liked it, or him.

He's cute, maybe, but ugh. Not really. You don't even recognise
when you feel revulsion for him that this is not the same

feeling as your near-constant disgust of yourself. It feels the same:
something's wrong with you and the world is normal.

Surely, though, once the 700 days are thousands of days
past, eventually, we'd be grown women, be in charge,

like in college! It would surely be better. Would turn
into the fun kind of love and romance and lust

that both the lovers liked! Leave way behind the New
Romantics, so embarrassing I even liked them,

and be cool enough to synthesise the harsher stuff,
the industrial clang of Ministry and New Order

with the warm/cold currents of R.E.M. and Everything
But The Girl, and the poetry and politics of Public

Enemy, the Beastie Boys' goofball misogyny rap
(being cool meant enduring those cruel lyrics if

you wanted to hang out) and Pixies obsession,
and pretending to like the Butthole Surfers,

swept away for real by L7 and K.D. and Ani
and Deee-Lite and the encroaching sponge of grunge.

So there were more options, plenty of ways
to get it right, right? Reggae, techno, rap, rock.

If a girl was good enough, and pretty enough, sexy
in the way that could earn the right kind of attention,

she might attract a guy who treated her special
as a complicated and exciting human being who

just happened to be sexy in the way that could
earn this right kind of attention.

This was the goal of the game.
This game with the vibe of a Roman gladiator stadium.

It was real life, this game, but you still had to play it.
If you won, you got to keep your body.

If you lost, you lost everything: your confidence,
your easy laughter, your ability to look in the mirror

and feel beautiful, your secret language, your eros,
your sense of humor, your flamboyant clothing style,

your enthusiasm for side-projects or for developing
your weaker arts, your lust, your late nights

alone without fear, your trust, your tipsy nights
dancing with friends, your friendships, your grades,

your way of flirting, your strange ability to shoot milk
out of your nose if there is sufficient social pressure,

your scholarship, your self-respect, your kindness,
your nights without nightmares, your openness,

your sense that you could choose or do what you wanted
and loved to do, your all and your future all.

Your dreams of having desire, believing that could
be relevant, and of fooling around, getting excited,

maybe falling for someone and wanting them,
and being wanted without being used by someone

who knows exactly how to use you.
Your story. The book of your life,

just the way you wanted to tell it, in the full
range of your voice. Your jumping, your singing,

your skating, your ranting, your shout of joy
in the sprinklers. That growing voice,

finding new timbre and tendency and tone.
Not just strong and smart but the chance

to quaver, too. Not just power—finding softness
and ambivalence and vigor and questions.

That voice, now rare, now quiet, keeps it in.
When it comes out, it's all question, all mark.

Your hope of being the brave and fierce
and loving and authentic protagonist

of the kind of story you wanted to read,
the story you wanted to live—none of that happened.

Or if it did, no one listened anyway, so why
say anything? But yours is not a story like this.

This is not a book anyone wants to read;
that's not a likable character, nothing she does

is believable. She's passive, lets herself
be a victim, where's her fire, her fight?

Why isn't she like Katniss, Hermione, Jo March,
Laura Ingalls, Lyra, Cowslip, Ramona, Heidi, Scout?

Unlike them, credible and realistic heroines,
she's not convincing. She's nothing like me.

Hers is not a voice you want to hear, nothing
she says matters, she's not a person you want

to have to listen to, page after page after page,
she's not real. I can't relate. She's not me,

171

she could never be me. That girl's long gone.
That girl didn't make it. No way that girl's

gonna make it. This isn't even a story.
My story's not here. Not even mine anymore—

I'm not even sure anything happened to me.
Or to whom everything happened.

Simone at Age 3, Late Summer

Total astonishment, 'Mommy! Look!
It's the moon!' Pointing to the silver

teacup glancing in blue late morning.
Then sternly: 'In the daytime.'

Her fingers cup her chin—a thinking
pose—she shakes her head solemnly

as if in disbelief, 'It's very, very strange.'
Looks at me again to confirm. 'Yes,

Simone, it's mysterious. Now come on,
let's move along. We gotta get to school.'

But she's still examining the sky. 'Look,'
I say, 'the leaves are just beginning to turn

brown and fall on the ground, see? That
means summer's almost over.'

'I like this breeze,' she says. 'I want
to stay here in the shade. You can have

the sun, Mommy. I know you like it.'
Protesting—'I like both'—I say, 'But let's

keep walking.' She sighs. 'This wind
is so nice'; she closes her eyes and follows

my voice, her big toes already reaching
the edges of her scuffed gold sandals.

They only lasted two months. Already she's
forgotten she'd meant to monitor the day

moon, and we might get to Court Street
on time, or nearly so. 'Summer's over,

the leaves fall in fall. The moon is strange,
very strange, but what season is the wind?'

Never Ever

Alarmed, today is a new dawn,
and that affair recurs daily like clockwork,

undone at dusk, when a new restaurant
emerges in the malnourished night.

We said it would be this way, once this became
the way it was. So in a way we were

waiting for it. I still haven't eaten, says the cook
in the kitchen. A compliant complaint.

I never eat, says the slender diner. It's slander,
and she's scared, like a bully, pushing

lettuce around. The cook can't look, blind with hunger
and anger. I told a waiter to wait

for me and I haven't seen him since. O it has been forty
minutes it has been forty years.

Late is a synonym for *dead*, which is a euphemism
for ever. Ever is a double-edged word,

at once itself and its own opposite: always
and always some other time.

In the category of *cleave*, then. To cut and to cling to,
somewhat mournfully.

That C won't let leave alone. Even so, forever's
now's never, and *remember* is just

the future occluded or dreaming. The day has come:
a dusty gust of disgusting August,

functioning as a people-mover. Maybe we're going
nowhere, wherever I go

I see us everywhere. On occasions of fanciness
or out to eat. As if people, stark, now-ish

people themselves were the forever of nothing,
the everything of nobody,

the very same self of us all, after all, at long
last the first.

FROM

The Octopus Museum

(2019)

Identity & Community (There Is No 'I' in 'Sea')

I don't want to be surrounded by people. Or even one person. But I don't
  want to always be alone.
The answer is to become my own pet, hungry for plenty in a plentiful place.
There is no true solitude, only only.
At seaside, I have that familiar sense of being left out, too far to glean the
  secret: *how go in?*
What an inhuman surface the sea has, always open.
I'm too afraid to go in. I give no yes.
Full of shame, but refuse to litter ever. I pick myself up.
Wind has power. Sun has power. What is power's source?

There's no privacy outside. We've invaded it.
There is no life outside empire. All paradise is performance for people who pay.
Perhaps I'm an invader and feel I haven't paid.
What a waste, to have lost everything in mind.

Watching there mom-like women try to go in, I'm green—I want to join them.
But they are not my women. I join them, apologising.
They splash away from me—they're their pod. People are alien.
I'm an unknown story, erasing myself with seawater.
There goes my honey and fog, my shoulders and legs.

What could be queerer than this queer tug-lust for what already is, who
  already am, but other of it?
Happens? That kind of desire anymore?
Of I am that queer thing pulling and greener than the blue sea. I'm new with
  envy.
Beauty washing over itself. No reflection. No claim. Nothing to see.
If there's anything bluer than the ocean it's is greenness. It's its turquoise
  blood, mixing me.

I was a woman alone in the sea.
Don't tell anybody, I tell myself.
Don't try to remmed this. Don't document it.
Remember: write down to not-document it.

No Traveler Returns

I was like you once, a sealed plastic bag of water filters floating on the sea.

I thought my numbers proved my time and space on earth.

I thought having children was a way of creating more love.

I thought thoughts I was ashamed to speak in case they were what everyone already thought or in case they were unthinkable thoughts nobody would dare think much less say which would blow up the world everyone else had to live in if I said them.

I muddled that distinction to extinction—pure silence not a piece of peace and a breathlessness not of wonder but blackthroat, choking on backwash.

Once a wild tentacled screaming creature every inch a kissed lip of a beloved place, a true and relentless mind, all heart if heart is a dumb hope of reusable pump.

What was it you said that made me think I was like you once?

Remember the last terrifying moments? You clenched up and wanted me to be completely open.

We'd broken up (remember such terms? Such luxury? We thought breaking up a kind of preservation.) and to cut off circulation decided to sever at the place where our hair had grown together.

An axe, a pair of kitchen scissors. That rusty axe fully fatigued and scissors which cut raw chicken bacteria into everything it touched.

Nothing did the trick. To come apart we'd have to come, together; and so I tried to make you come; you said it was our last time so you'd remember it.

You cried out, then cried and I cried and I hardened against you, then softened, then wished we could go back, wanted to love you like before, twisted myself like nobody's pile of wires.

Did you try to make me come, and I couldn't, wouldn't? Or did I give you that and let you let me go?

———————

And there will be no other way to be, once this way's gone. The last song on earth, the last jellybean. Last because nobody wanted it, or everybody sang it, till the end.

Once this day in November's over never another. Each day nothing like the last except that it's the last and that's new, too.

Each moment broken glasses, a covered mirror, foxed. The waste stays in place. The rest disappears. The unrest, too.

There's no way to follow my own mind. My own mind is not leading. I'm unleaded. I'm gasoline.

I'm everything in between this flame and that attracted wind. I forgot my glasses—how will we drink?

Seeing isn't believing if I believe I see better with something I can so easily forget.

And what if I can't forget? I forgot the heft and squirm of my own baby in my arm, in my own womb.

I'll forget anything and call it an accident, match to fuel and breathing it all in as if I'm living normally from day to re-registered day.

Why is it, if I can only remember what I myself experienced, that I can also forget what I experienced? Who records the records and collects the recollections?

181

I had that baby in my womb for thirty-nine weeks, for three quarters of a year, a full calendar minus summer. An unforgettable summer, each day fucking endless.

Oh I know all the numbers; everything adds up. I've never seen my womb but my doctor has. I never saw that doctor again.

Gift Planet

My six-year-old said, 'I don't know time.' She already knows it's unknowable. Let it be always a stranger she walks wide around.

I fantasise about outer space as if I have some relation to it besides being an animal in its zoo. No visitors. No matter how far I travel on earth I wind up sitting in rooms.

Wind up running all over towns and streets the same. Then get hungry as anywhere, again. Going anyplace, I think: I never want to go home and I can't wait to be home.

All traveling's a way to imagine having a home to leave or return to.

The shame of never leaving home. The anguish of no home. Changing housekeys on the unchanged ring. The ring is the home, the thing inside trees.

Claiming a tree 'mine"

Car feels like a pod, an exoskeleton, a place inside me. Car short for 'carapace'.

I blame the weather, blame myself if the weather is 'nice'. Tell myself the weather ruined my plans, though it's me ruined the weather's.

Plan: like plane like plain like pain/pane. Like planet. Plan acting like an overlay on everything most elemental. Trying to make everything go according to it—feelings, food, flight, ordinariness, the very earth.

Stop already. Stop as if you can. As if you can breathe back in your own baby, your two, your three. Breathe out all the ones you never had. Breathe in one two three. Breathe out all the others.

I don't want to be cremated. I want to be part of earth. Space may be my original home but I only remember here.

I cling to this life. I've taped myself to it like a card on a gift. Happy birthday! Many happy returns and hope it's lots of fun! We miss you! Love, Me.

A gift is always an exchange of energy. Like water boiling, like photosynthesis. Inside the box is a water pitcher and a picture of us together as we were when the photo was taken.

Now it's given. It's only a copy, but the original was a moment and was burned up, caloric.

Simone says before bed, 'I'm imagining a strawberry automatically drawn. I dream so much when I'm awake.'

When I learned to tell time I told it. I told it so; I stopped listening to what it tried to tell me: You're already losing everything as you go and go and go.

There Was No Before (Take Arms Against a Sea of Troubles)

Before health insurance there was health, a pre-existing condition before the weird paper-cut-on-the-neck had you eventually getting around in a wheelbarrow pulled by a gentle mule named Sinister. Sure it's metaphoric. Also true.

When I say you, I mean me. Who else can I talk to? Before you were born, the world got along hopelessly without you, lonely without even knowing why. The sharp edges of birdsong scraped across the sky gay with fever, no way to bring it down.

On the ground, houses were called homes and homes were called living spaces and they dotted the sick countryside—those near-dead spaces. Dead spaces were called cemeteries back then, too. Dead air was what the interred watched on TV.

Everything was a show, which must go on and on, continuing in sleep rehearsal space. In the morning our dreams were still a mess, nobody knew the blocking, gels melted onto the hot lights, and we could hardly sit through the thing.

In waking life we said our lines or broke character or looked directly at the lens, and were entertained. We binge-watched ourselves till we believed daybreak was a rerun and the stars a quiet new kind of crime drama that had inaudible singing in it.

My child would complain when I didn't let her stay the second half of the pre-school day. 'I want to be part of the Lunch Bunch!' though I'd make her her favorite at home. Of course the school had to make it sound fun for kids to be left all day.

I couldn't afford all-day pre-school. Soon nobody could afford it. Before and after-Before, too. Children have always had to stuff their whole selves into the corners pinning their grown-ups. I thought I'd miss her too much anyway, and indeed I do.

I know nothing about her job these days. Surely she's got a lunch bunch at the staff caf with her break mates. A corner of her own with friends before her second shift. She has so little time outside of work.

Before Sinister came into the family you rolled yourself down, saying *It's all downhill from here*. Which was the same as saying *It's all uphill*. You'd pick up friends, neighbors, exes, along the way and give them rides. You all went downhill fast.

Black children were killed in broad daylight, in parks and streets and in houses and churches and cars. Especially in cars. The law said it wasn't allowed, but it was expressly allowed, encouraged, and unpunished. The law said this was the law, each time a person chose to do it. These were not accidents.

This was Before, and we're almost certain it is the same now as Before, only now we don't know the laws. They keep it overtly secret now, as they think we'll think there was no Before. It's not just black children anymore, it's everyone.

We didn't all used to have shells. Our skin was soft and easily cut, even a sheet of paper could sever your nerves, become infected, and leave you wheelbarrow-bound. It didn't even matter what was written on the paper.

We could afford our naked flesh, survival-wise, less so if the outer layer of your flesh was dark or part-dark. And there were commonly awful injuries to the softest flesh especially of women and kids where men turned their flesh to weapons.

These were not accidents. These injuries altered the bodies and minds of the women and kids and changed the flesh and spirit of the as-yet uninjured, too. The threat of flesh harming flesh went beyond flesh.

Because it was the mind of a person that put the harm in motion. A person chose to do it. Women hid in basements, trying to imagine the mind of a man bent on harm. Kids thought they had to do whatever the grownups told them.

They thought that a man who had a puppy was always nice. Women swaggered in groups downtown and were picked off one by one. Women thought they were the only one every time it happened. Kids stopped remembering whole years.

———————

Long before people existed, mollusks were soft plasmic shapes for whom, if you mentioned shells they'd say *Whatever you're talking about is completely alien to me and I am not interested* as if you were trying to sell them, simple Ediacaran bilateral, a bridge.

After millions of years of disinterested, shell-less floating and sea-floor-attaching, they only developed shells in response to a new scene in the oceans. Predators became invented and the undersea nobodies strategised with zero brains.

The 'new' predators were the first on earth, the first dog to eat dog in this world. Mollusks grew shells, homes and stayed inside for millions more years, sometimes daring to stick a foot out, footing around for food.

You see these shells on the beach. Or you did before, when we walked on the beach free as birds plucking innards. They are decorative, sheeny little half-compacts—each a grim acquiescence to a new regime, and the first resistance.

When my grandma was little she heard the maxim 'It's a dog-eat-dog world' as 'It's a doggy dog world.' Oh little grandma! Before mollusks were forced to grow shells it was doggy-dog out there. But ever since then we're hungry all the time.

We also dream of multiple-ingredient meals. Carrots for dinner two nights a week is not what we imagined when we thought we chose Vegan Paradise, or before when we believed in the feelings of animals but still ate them with relish, hot sauce, mustard, and regret.

We envisioned rainbow salads with cream-free goddess dressing, long, funky grains of every stripe mixed with soups of the world, not a medium-large can of beets per family as a treat on Tuesdays. Fridays we get beans and whatever lettuce is lying around. Bitter stems, semi-liquid.

Before, we could always count on at least a heel or two of gluten loaf, but it depends on which cruelty-full Before you're thinking of. Me, I'm thinking of all the Befores, like all old people who have no future.

Before our COO learned how to communicate electronically, we thought they were merely naively excited about 'life on land' (LOL) so we equally naively helped them build COOPS (Cephalo-Octopodal Oceanostomy Pods).

Soon we realised we'd been doubly naive and they'd been zero naive because they used their new land mobility to access the world's Electronic Communication Operating Systems (ECOS) and boy could they type fast.

It became clear that they, the COO (Cephalopod Octopoid Overlords) were taking over. While we were still marveling at the cuteness of YouTube videos showing early COO antics and enjoying the adorableness of their eight-legged smartypants brand,

they had reconfigured the ECOS language, and took over every computer, grid, and control center. We still do not know their language. We think they think we are too stupid to learn it and we know they know they are probably right.

COO read, or rather ingested, the entire internet in a matter of weeks. Who knew their decentralised nervous system, advanced visual acuity, and eight highly sensitive mega-arms would make such quick work in the realm of keystrokes and swipe commands?

It's almost as if we invented this technology to play to their specific evolutionary strengths. They have complex, light-sensitive, four-dimensional, laser vision and we have 20/20 hindsight.

The COO renamed itself the CEO (Cephalopod Electro-Overlords)— dropping the *Octopus* nickname as an outdated, human-centric, offensive term that excluded the squid, nautiluses, and other potential commanding officers and executives-in-training.

Likewise, COOPS are now called COPS, installed in watchtowers and moats in every human settlement. Most of us work in their salinising centers. Before, we dumped our waste and garbage into their oceans, and ruined that delicate world.

Their vast home of millions of years destroyed, the COO came ashore. We knew they were intelligent. They could open jars and pretend to be more poisonous creatures than they, ostensibly, were. We found them darling, delicious.

They don't understand our racism. They change color and blend in. To them, change is only ever considered a natural gift, a condition of being. The real skill is survival. Knowing how to change—not color or mind or body or action but perspective—and refusing to do it is how species vanish.

My shell has become relatively substantial—proportionate to the amount of danger I'm in. I'm a woman. A mother. I am very soft and have so much to protect. Many women and mothers, even the old and weak, have the strongest shells.

Except for certain pale women who were extremely wealthy Before. They seem to lack a certain enzyme. Their shells are transparent, bendable, a vinyl-like film, but porous like all they can grow and carry on their backs is a flimsy safety net.

Mine's a cross between hardwood and Corian, the plastic-stone stuff they used to make slightly cheaper kitchen counters. Of course it's not really made of those materials. It's made of me. Thick-middled, silver-streaked, motherfucking furious me.

I don't know about men's shells. They won't tell me and I don't care enough to care. Maybe I blame them for all the years of cluelessness and rampage. Or I'm ashamed of us all and prefer to think mostly about my daughter, how she's getting by.

Bakamonotako

I was thinking of changing my name to Bakamonotako. It meant The Stupid Little Octopus Girl, she was a character from an old Japanese folk tale. I read her story on a plaque outside the Little Sea Monster Museum Sculpture Garden. I thought she was a lot like me.

From a good family of upstanding octopi, Bakamonotako felt she did not need her eight appendages, she only needed four. Two to wash and work and two to walk and wander.

To the embarrassment and horror of her family, she let her other four limbs fall into such disuse that they withered and fell away. So she resembled a human being, with two arms, two legs, except that her mouth and genitalia were the same orifice.

Like all stupid little girls who believe they can best become themselves by being unlike themselves, she eventually came to miss her lost limbs. At times, fully tattooed people feel so about their lost original skin.

When Bakamonotako matured and tried to have sexual relations as an adult octopus, the limbs she cast off with her mind wrapped around her and bound her, keeping her from any feeling.

Embittered and maddened by this, she consulted a wise starfish about her future. The starfish said 'You must find the other half of yourself, of your private and deepest feeling, and you might have to double yourself to do it.'

The starfish asked Bakamonotako for twice her usual fee for this advice, and the stupid little octopus girl paid half in sand dollars and half in sand dollars she hoped to collect in the future.

With only half her limbs, she would need to spend twice as much time scrambling in the sand on the ocean floor to find these dollars. She could see already how her fate of constantly halving and doubling was playing itself out, never to be whole, clear, even.

She had spent half her future already, searching for sand dollars to pay the starfish for advice about her future, which had already been determined by her past.

'At this rate,' thought Bakamonotako, 'I'll spend my whole life looking backwards, neither living nor not living. Unless I can figure out how to accomplish the seemingly impossible task set forth by the wise starfish.'

G-Bread

One of my indulgences was going to the Gingerbread House some evenings, sitting gingerly in a little gingerbread chair to eat the best g-bread. For saturation and when I could splurge the money. I felt him, one day, peeking in the sugar-frosted windows but of course he did not come in.

Perhaps he was intimidated by how intimate the place is. Too small to sit comfortably really. Or maybe by how good I smelled in it, the spice sweat-sauna ripened me as a brown paper back will sweeten out the mealiest pear.

On religious days, of which there are many but few for me, I went to the Temple of the Three Mouths. I fed all three what they were hungry for, which took some guesswork and often-sketchy improvisations. Whatever the three mouths requested became a kind of omen for me.

Mouth One, the mouth of physicality, was the easiest. Once, it wanted peanut sauce, which made sense because it likes protein and viscosity, form and content. Mouth two twice puzzled me, once wanting a blue video and once wanting to lick my arm!

This being the mouth of love I wondered why it wanted such silly forms of it and could only guess that I came to it with deformed notions and therefore could only offer it debased versions of what I most wanted. Still, it made me sad.

The third mouth I gave whatever I could barely keep from gobbling up myself. Chocolate tomatoes and books I couldn't sleep for. Oils and petals and commotions I dreamt of on my luckiest nights. And the mouth would have none of it. I was refused every time. The mouth of abandonment.

I thought this mouth meant something and then that something was inverse. I was always baffled. Until I could penetrate the mystery, make the third mouth desire what I have to give, I would continue my supplications at the Temple.

My religious days were generally those days when my own company turned against me, when I couldn't stand myself a minute longer. What my visits to the Temple did to assuage this in-skin repulsion I don't know—and it only half-works. It was a form of religion after all.

But, after I returned home, I felt a relief, a snake in the middle of its shedding, knowing there was still this cylinder of self left.

Sel de la Terre, Sel de Mer

Oh funny, runny little god who lived in the sea we cut to ribbons! Tell us the big story with your infected mouth. Tell us the big story is so far beyond us we can't possibly ruin it, but you'll let us listen if we sit way in the back, quiet side creatures and marginal beasts.

We don't know what we're doing. We catch a single wave, bless you with necklaces of spit, strut ashore to pose with our medallions and titles, having won. We make little boats and toss ourselves inside like a ride on a mechanical bull. When thrown we blame the weather.

We can't see anything in front of our face. Salt water stings and burns our eyes even when we're already crying. We cover them with plastic goggles to ogle each other underwater. We know we are aliens in too deep, but we'll never admit we don't belong.

We are the kind of storytellers that frustrate children at bedtime everywhere. 'Once there was a little girl named [insert name] who was very tired and went to sleep. The end.' Come on! 'Okay, one more story. Once upon a time there was a blanket that was so lonely.

Its great wish was to one day cover up a little girl named [insert name]. Finally, after what seemed like forever and was actually way past 8:30 p.m., the girl came to bed, pulled up her blanket all cozy, and went to sleep. The end.' But you can't pull one over on kids, who know when they're shorted.

Our only ways are the scammy, power-tripping ways and we know we don't deserve it but we want to hear the big story. We need an old-fashioned plume of ink, all new alphabet, to blot out our lies, all the times we were too tired, unkind, and stupid to tell the truth.

All day a rainy day so we stay inside. That's how we see things: we close our eyes twice. That's how afraid we are of what is. When the rain stops, we dive into pools of plastic water, mistake the sexual fingers of light for fullness of heart, for the goodness of our own gooey center.

We thought we were so smart, always ahead of ourselves, minds flapping like a single flag, a mere reaction, a neural blip we thought was holy everywhere. Make us sit and listen to you. If you're at the center the center might hold.

Your countless eyes watching us, your arms radiating out in all directions, feeling for what's next. Sound comes to us in waves and we dissolve into salt water when we're most real.

Thinking Lessons

No one is one.
No one is no one.

Is writing an act of listening?
  Or is to *listen* merely to passively search another for a portal to oneself?
    But *portal* lets anything through—and nothing stays.

I love what's sublime—beauty greater than my sense of beauty.

Red is the color of surfacing, from the inside, eyes closed.

My child does not belong to me. She belongs to herself. But she's too young to have a child!

What is a new way to learn? Could I ever answer and still keep my question?

What are the most important questions, other than this one?

Our Beloved Infinite Crapulence

In Indiana, in the era of hell-wealth, way past deadline, someone on the account is sweating it, making metaphor from what is already a stretch.

And because he wants to go home to his farm-fresh slowpoke foam, grown cold, we are eventually diagnosed with winter and treated to this marketing copy off a tube of cream: 'Undry Your Skin' or 'A Rainforest for Your Face'.

I bought it. It seemed fresh and felt organic and like it would at least wetten me, skinwise. I can't feel my old ambition to be wracked with anguish or to grow soft with loss.

When I lose, I'm still so graceful! Does that make me a chump or a champ, eating victory mussels in the lamplight of my domestic tranquility?

Gratitude often leaves me with nothing to say, as when I saw you in the toy store, I felt like a feral cat who knows only the dumpsters and the flu-scented sandboxes of now. Now that I'm happy I suppose I have to break my own heart just to feel something.

Another person with my same name goes around impersonating others; now everyone thinks I'm the impostor.

I want to tell her, 'you know, you think you know me, sipping mahogany cider in the millionaire's billiards room, but there's such a thing as too much umami, and there's no way to rest forever and then go on.'

Someone once said: now that I'm happy I suppose I have to break my own heart to feel something. I should remember that. I should stop praying to my dead self.

I should pull out my earbuds, and hear the world (my first love, my favorite store) without continually moving my oiled jaw hinge.

I like a chemical mysticism performed with perfect innocence. The wet slit lit up and cut down the middle, a little spit, lip a little bit split. Love in the Candle Shop: Wicked. Peeing into a Plastic Water Bottle: Wasteful. These are scents.

As in: Luck Be a Lady, So Spend Your Whole Social Security Check on Lottery Tickets Be a Gentleman. I want to smell like ceramic wind in the canyon, a brittle lust, a red-headed remedy synonymous with flooding.

Weathervane Rusted Stuck. A Stranger's Phalanges. The South Mouth. Fiercely Phlegm. Fun Old Lady. So Parachute!

And now we eat. The eponymous eating. Don't want butter, don't want salt. Dinner is thinner but it's not my fault. We're having fungal celebrity of beef cheeks tomorrow so get yourself hungry!

For lighter fare I prefer the Soapish Fish braised in its own frothing broth, served with an aromatic retraction of statements previously made in the shade of a giant, genetically-muddled-with fiddlehead fern, infused with expelled chipmunk breath.

I... I love this local company, especially because for every order—and this is so cool—they make a tax-deductible contribution to honor and support the world-famous Pacific Garbage Patch, in your name.

Blueberries for Cal

Watching little Henry, six, scoop up blueberries
and shove them into his mouth, possessed.

I'm so glad I brought blueberries—wish my kids
could/would eat them. Cal can't; Simone won't.

Henry's sisters Lucy & Jane took turns feeding each
other goldfish crackers and sips of juice.

Arms around each other's neck and back. Tiny things.
I wish my daughter had a sister like that

and my son a nervous system that let him walk
and munch berries. Sometimes I can't bear

all the things Cal doesn't get to do. I want to curse
everything I can't give him.

Admire/compare/despair—that's not the most real
feeling I'm feeling, is it? I feel joy in Henry's joy.

Blueberries for the child who wants them.
There's all this energetic sweetness, enough to go around,

to give and taste and trust. More than enough,
For Cal, too. I want to remember this.

My children seem to subsist on music and frosting.
Whee there's frosting, there's cake.

Where there's music, someone chose to make a song
over all other things on this earth.

Are Women People?

A report commissioned by the COP's Department of Human Studies. In the interest of anthropological authenticity, cephalopod researchers utilised only methods and modes used by humans themselves, in their various legal, academic, and socio-cultural institutions. To the best of our ability, we worked within their language and wielded their tools in order to better understand their mysteries, and how to serve mankind's legacy. — the authors

1 *Framing Thoughts:*

We don't believe the question in the report's title to be self-evident.

Governing documents use this term, *self-evident*, so it seems legit, foundational, but it's a pleonasmic tautology, a proud cheese full of holes, a question answered untruly by itself, palindrome-like: Is it real? Real it is!

To begin to understand how to answer the question we must define the two terms: *women* and *people*. *People* is a broader term than *women*. Women are a subset of people. Women are a kind of people.

People are not a kind of women.

At this moment someone will always say: men are also a subset of people! It goes the other way, too! People who need to interject that point are usually men. When you hypothetically posit the word *women* as a term that includes men (logical, as the word *men* is already there within the word *women*) in practice the terms lose all meaning.

Men found it insulting and risky not to be named as the sole primary term—it seemed wrong, their personhood status implied but not fully legally inscribed. And it was deemed too clunky to have to say *men and women* every single time a reference was made to people, so *women* became the secondary term, an addendum to the word *men*.

To recap: People includes both men and women. *Man* claims to include women, but doesn't. *Woman* doesn't include men, or women as a group. *Man* is plural, encompassing humanity (which, clearly, serves man). *Woman* is singular, individual. To each her own.

Does a person have to be a human being?
Are animals people?
Are corporations people?
Are ideas people?
Are objects made by humans people?
Are fictional characters people?

What about past people?
Are dead people still people?
Are people who exist in memory only, names inscribed on stones on buildings, people?
Are people who only exist in wills and legal terms people?
Are the wishes and requests of dead people people?
Are ghosts, once they've been proven to exist, people?

What about future people?
Are children people?
Are babies people?
Are unborn babies people?
Are fetuses people?
Are embryos people?
Are zygotes people?
Are sperm people?
Are ova people?
Are people's plans to have children people?
Are the ova of people's children people?
Are the ova of people's unborn babies people?
Are the ova of fetuses people?
Are the ova of embryos people?
Are the undifferentiated cells that may become ova or sperm people?
Are the undifferentiated cells that may become people who may become parents to people who may become parents to people who may become parents to people who many becomes parents people?

If there's a possibility that essential parts (undifferentiated cells, for example) of people are in themselves also people, then are other essential parts also people?

Is a human brain people?

Is a human heart people?

Is human waste people?

Is human emotion people?

Is human ingenuity people?

Is human survival instinct people?

Is the basic luck to be born at all people?

Is DNA people?

Is a torso people?

Is a neck people?

If it's possible that essential parts are people, might non-essential parts be people?

Is a foot people?

Are seeing or unseeing eyes people?

Is human sexual arousal people?

Is a human sense of humor people?

Is language people?

Is talent people?

Are mental disorders people?

Are diseases people?

Is a photograph that captures the essences of a person and allows that person to live on in human memory people? (i.e., a child pointing to a photo, saying, 'That's Grandma!')

What about people for whom essential or non-essential parts are absent? Are they people? Are parts of them people, but not other parts? Is it possible to be part people/part non-people?

Are humans with artificial body parts people?

Are humans who hurt other humans without remorse people?

Are humans who cannot take care of themselves people?

Are humans who are chemically dependent people?

Are humans who are terminally ill people?

Are humans who lack melanin people?

Are humans who lack compassion people?

Are humans who have impaired function (physical, mental, emotional) people?

Are humans who do not use language people?

Are humans who could survive in the wild with no human interaction people?
Are loners people?
Are people who can't learn people?
Are people who don't want to learn people?

Are people who hold positions of power in governance, law enforcement,
  or other hierarchies that control the lives and freedom of people people?
Are members of Congress people? (Is the State people?)
Are police people? (Is the embodiment of law enforcement, to which people
  must submit, people?)
Are scientists people? (Is someone first and foremost beholden to the data
  people?)
Are engineers/programmers who only work with machines, never humans,
  people? (Are machines people?)
Are dancers people? (Are humans who primarily use their bodies for art
  people?)
Are artists people? (Is someone for whom aesthetic questions are primary
  people?)

3 *Special Status: Children*

Children are, at the very least, future people, but anything could happen.

They could be female, and a good half of them do end up as such, so
children are just as likely to become future women (not people) as they are
to become people.

They could belong to a religion, and depending on which one, this might
make them god's people, not people-in-themselves. For example: the
Christian god in particular does not share, so Christians are not people,
they are god's.

In the case of Buddhists, their god shares them and they share their god,
but as they share themselves with everyone and all, belonging to none—
not even themselves—they cannot be claimed as, or to be, people.

There are many such cases to be considered.

Depending on geography or parental heritage, having brown or dark skin, skin which does not usually change even over a long life, these factors...

these factors, in and of themselves, have no bearing on whether or not they are people...

but in certain circumstances present obstacles
to their inclusion

Mere origin or heritage or skin color is not in and of itself considered a factor

and in the case of mixed-heritage, or dual-country-of-origin, there are complexities

to consider the fixities of legal terms, to honor existing definitions where they do exist

Let it be stated that People of Color, taking into account all of the variables and contingencies, are certainly people (unless they are women or future people—a separate category with variables and contingencies as argued above and below).

These people are a category in and of themselves—a kind of people obligated to continually renew their licenses, registrations, residencies, identification papers, passports, bank account information, school enrollment, property deeds or rental leases, birth and death certificates, health benefits, medical forms and records, utility accounts, social security data, employment records, political party affiliations.

These documents must be continually updated to protect the status of People of Color as people.

These documents are and records are proof that dark-skinned people, brown people, people who come from Countries of Color or who have one or more parents from Countries of Color are people, and it is incumbent upon them to keep all records and data updated, renewed, and accurate.

This is all for their own protection.

There is a long history of fraudulence, misinformation, identity theft, impersonation, money laundering, forged documents, improper resignation, multiple claims, and other illegal activity, so vigilance is required to protect People of Color's status as people.

Legal offenses, such as criminal activity and association with violence, can result in the individuals forfeiting their access to this system of registration and renewal required to extend their status as people in perpetuity. If individuals enter the prison or corrections systems as perpetrators of crimes, they can no longer uphold the obligation of being people, and the status of personhood can be revoked.

Outside the judicial and correctional systems, it's possible to default on that status as well. Simply forgetting to renew registration or any of the above documents can render questionable/null/void an individual's status in the group known as people. Crimes are defined as any 'illegal activity' and this includes any lapses in registrations or expired documents.

5 *Reproductive Functions and Management of Men and Women*

Differences between men and women are primarily physical. Socialisation, legislation, education, and segregation have codified, altered, and enhanced those physical differences, it seems, in the interest of the people.

1. People are physically born out of the bodies of women.
2. Male sperm are required to start new human life, but sperm can be separated from men, stored indefinitely, used at will, without any need for the rest of the physical man.
3. Female ova can also be harvested, frozen, implanted separately from the woman, but no artificial replacement has been found for the gestation of the embryo. This forty-week period of gestation can only occur in the body of a living woman. There is currently no medical or scientific research advocating the creation of artificial gestational systems.

4. Women are required to make People.
   (a) this has been interpreted in two ways
      (i) 'women, inseparable from their bodies, are essential to making people.'
      (ii) 'women are obligated/compelled to make people'
5. Men are not required to make people.
   (a) this has been interpreted in two ways
      (i) 'men, whose reproductive contribution is easily and painlessly extractable from their bodies, are inessential to making people'
      (ii) 'men are not obligated/compelled to make people'
6. People are dependent on women to continue making people. Such a small percentage of women are (1) of child-bearing age, (2) able to bear children, and (3) want to bear children. Some estimate that only 7–10% of the total population are women who meet all three criteria to bear children.
7. For the benefit of all people to ensure their survival and continuation of the human species, women's reproductive systems—inasmuch as they are inseparable from women as beings—are of collective special interest to the people, and can be said to be 'held in trust' of the people.
8. For survival and continuation of the people themselves, the people are the Trustees of the reproductive capacities of women between the ages of thirteen and fifty. Women of childbearing age and ability cannot be said to have full control over their bodies, as they may not qualify as Trustees, if they are not proven to be people.
9. This document seeks to discover whether women can be proven to be people.
10. In the event that proof cannot be obtained that women are people, women will be held indefinitely (or until proof can be obtained) in a 'pre-status' category. 'Pre-status' status confers no rights of people-hood, which are deferred until the required documentation is obtained, received, and validated.

6 *Conclusion*

Based on our research, it appears the definition of 'human' is unstable, and so is that of the plural synonym of 'people'. Human parts may or may not be 'people' and as 'women' are a part of the term 'people' they may or may not qualify in and of themselves. It has been discovered that a tiny minority of humans can legally, fully occupy the category of people (with most of the population falling into the subcategories of Special Status and Women) and this minority is deeply endangered, growing more minuscule as time passes. It has been established that women are occasionally people, depending on circumstances that can change. This is primarily because they are essential to the survival of the human species and therefore they paradoxically are (1) the seat, crux, and essence of people as well (2) too essential in their reproductive capacity to be allowed full personhood— their bodies must be held in trust by the state (which confers personhood) in pre-status from ages thirteen to fifty in order to preserve the future of potential people. In the cases that women are also in 'Special Status' categories as people of color and/or children, further contingencies apply.

Our Zero Waiver

Her head in my lap, looking up at the sky. I watched her face watch the stars, moon lighting her like a still lake. I couldn't tell what color her eyes were; they could be light ordinarily but collected all the dark tickets to ride the night in peace, in calm, tonight.

I brushed her hair away from her forehand. I don't think she's happy, but her worries have smoothed, it seems. How could she be happy? She came to us under an inhuman law and I have no idea what she suffered. She's somewhere between thirty-eight and forty-two, and she had nowhere to go.

We took her in. We don't have much but we couldn't bear the feeling of hoarding our one extra bedroom, since Nana died. We figured we'd volunteer for a minus-one/plus-one Zero Waiver, instead of waiting and watching the household rations be cut due to decreased household size.

No, we aren't so selfless a family. I'll never know if we would have been. If things were different, would we have taken in foster children, adopted orphaned or abandoned babies? Opened our doors, arms aching to give love where love was needed?

Instead of waiting for them to reassess our unit, for them to size us up for an assigned new occupant, we figured if we volunteered at least we could choose the category. That way we'd be assigned a woman between the ages of thirty-eight and forty-two (there's a surplus).

I was mostly worried we'd get assigned an Offender. A man. Someone who lied and broke down doors and would keep us sleepless. We couldn't choose who'd come to live with us but we could avoid an Offender if we took on an Early Crone.

We were allowed an EC because we're not allowed another non-Offender man. It's why we couldn't take in our friend Paul, who needed a home. Our old neighbor Michelle could have been safe with us but she's too young. Until age thirty she'll live in the Young Women's Space.

You get someone who doesn't know you, usually from another town. Someone who probably has to leave for any of the usual reasons—a baby is born or a family member is released back into the home. Sometimes it's her own baby. Sometimes a sibling returns.

There are unofficial 'occupancy-matchmakers' more broker than seer. They know many people in a lot of single-family-occupancy housing, and folks tell them the news, the comings and goings. Welch was our broker.

We gave her daughter reading lessons for a year as soon as Nana got sick, payment in advance for finding us a good woman of the right age and circumstance. It was almost too much to hope for to find someone remotely stable or sane. Show me one person who is these days—that's a clone.

She brought Amy to our place one week ago. Amy's been crying a lot, and then stone-faced, and then apologetic, her misery genuine, her smile forced. She must have had a baby she had to leave, or the baby died. In any case, her milk came in.

My heart broke for her. Nobody's allowed to waste baby milk but fuck it—not everything can be salvaged, inventoried, sold. Together we went out to the back yard near the trees and lay down on our backs. I didn't want to touch her. How tender she must be.

But she propped her head onto the pillow of my lap, better to see the stars and moon. I sat up then, better to watch her. My skirt was wet in two spots from her tears. Her shirt was wet in two spots from her milk. My own cheeks were streaked, my eyes mirrored, shadowed, by her shining ones.

The night was celebrating its sparkles, moonglow, glimmering, showing off like TV shows used to show themselves at night, exposing themselves in our living rooms. She and I made no sound, said nothing. What could we say? Who could hear it in that loud night flashing its millions of bodies?

Our Family on the Run

Everything organised around Cal in his wheelchair. He can't walk and I can't carry him far. We'd have the wheelchair van, as long as we could find gas. Simone in the side seat, Craig and me in the front.

Maybe spray paint a Super Soaker metallic silver to make it look like a real weapon?

Load the car up with cans of enteral food for Cal's G-tube. Maybe a six-week supply, plus a go-backpack full of cans, extensions, spare Mic-Key button. Three days of food for the rest of us. We'll find water.

Sleeping in the front seats, taking turns on watch. Simone curled up next to the gas can and ziplock of batteries/cords/chargers, with her one stuffed animal we have to worry about something happening to, her only toy.

And what if we lose the car? Running on some side road to—Pennsylvania/airport/Atlantic/evacuation center/relocation camp/as yet unknown. Trying to buy a blow-up raft for four people. Can't take the wheelchair.

Our stack of euros to buy four plane tickets: can't take the wheelchair.

On foot, trying to get to a friend's country home, promise of a bedroom. No way to call the friend for directions. A compass one of the kids got at a birthday party wound up under a car seat. Lucky.

Lucky, too, Simone can walk—though she gets tired and I'd want to hoist her on my back if I didn't have to save my energy to carry Cal when Craig's legs give way, his back out.

Cal, four foot six and sixty pounds of tween, who must be carried if we somehow lose that wheelchair. Or the wheelchair breaks, or is stolen, or gets a flat tire, or rusts.

It's red, a color Cal chose by smiling when we said 'red' in a list of colors. No expression when we said blue, green, black, purple, or pink. Big smile when we said red. He had his choice and he made it.

How strange that the color of his wheelchair ever mattered enough to anyone to offer him that handful of options.

Simone is hungry. I give her a Clif bar (that twenty-four pack I bought for rushed mornings) and she drops half of it on the dirt road, which is covered in, what, bone dust or atomised drywall?

She grabs what she dropped and stuffs it into her mouth before I can stop her. Why would I stop her?

The side of the road is the well-known gutter of desperation always included in stories about wars where many people have to move on foot to the next terrible place.

No matter what the emergency, whenever people are forced to flee you find, piece by piece, how their understanding of their situation changed.

If you read the stories, you're supposed to find abandoned photo albums, suitcases, babies. The useless things cut out by survival's swift knife. Dead weight, long gone.

You never find food, bottled water, working flashlights, live batteries, shortwave radios. It's true, what all those stories said, it turns out.

Eventually out of water and arms shredded, I carry Cal, Craig carries me, and Simone carries all of us. Almost seven years old, she is so strong and has some Clif bars stuffed in a bag. The notebook with all our information is long lost.

She knows where she's going. How does she know that? She runs ahead and carries us, her heart pounding and breaking with the weight and strain of all of us in there.

New Poems

Moving Far Away

I hear they're trying to make borders in water now,
to declare it a place, impose a shape,
dissolve the solvent.

It's no solution to our probable problem:
I'll never see you again, I say on my cell. Said
to myself. We'll be well below alone now.

Can I be a good friend to you if I move so far away?
Haven't seen you in years but I like a rough edge—
island broken off a big bully,

I'll use up all my firewood on you.
Sorcery, what turned into me?
An iron foot, a leg of log. A wish for symmetry.

My fire handed down to me by cauldron witches
in their longish unauthorised youth—
broken crest rising,

rinsed of desire, full of pull and push no rush
to finish or to vanish. As if water didn't wave,
and bring tidings,

and answer me like an animal
jealous, crushed, washing herself.
I'll never forget you told me never to forget

but I did. Your voice a needle threaded
heading for my open wound,
already burned clean for a clean split.

The Impossible Lesbian Love Object(s)

(after Meret Oppenheim, Hélène Cixous & Gertrude Stein)

1

It's just an object, it's not me.

I'm more than an object, we are not having tea.

I am not one, not two. I am a feminist three.

I am Dada—not Mama, never will be.

When no one can use me, I am most free.

2

I am not like other objects unaware
of themselves, those props subbing for desire:

the corner of the room thinks the room is one-cornered,
that cat sculpture staring as if with its eyes.

I too am a mammal stolen from my original sense of thirst.
Women know this disappearance from meaning.

Like all lesbian triptychs, I've stumbled.
Like all love objects, I am triangular, unstable.

I'm a lonely trio, a single setting, vexed
and passive, sexed and distracted.

A hot drink, a pot on the fire, the muscles
loosened, an inner stirring, a little spill,

the coat on the floor. The fur coat on the floor.
The curved fur floor atop another fur circle

to never catch a drop and a concave face
with convex back, swirling nothing.

None of it really happening.
I was once and always only ever an idea,

just a clever blip, a quip, a dare,
converted by coin and concept,

given body, shape, hair,
and an immortal uselessness

all art thinks it's born with,
that women can't get near.

3

I'm beloved for being art's best worst idea.
Famous for being impossible,

that's why I'm obscene.
Not because everybody wants to fuck the cup,

not even the spoon can get it up.
Full frontal frottage, sapphic saucer,

a curving inside-outness, hairy leather hole.
Liquid's skill is soaking, then getting sucked.

Seed's luck is spilling, then being tilled.
It turns out we are having tea,

but it's all so heavy with life-cycles
that even when you go light, with art,

to get a little air, the room's still a bit dark.
And I'm repulsed, which attracts, in fact

the promise of warm fur is ancient,
will outlast the ritual fire and water

of tea for three, not two.
You see there's me, and you, and we.

Pelts melt into a new body, not old.
We're not thirsty—we're not cold.

4

I'm not just an object,
my surfaces servicing,
but I'm no more than myself.

I end at my edges, finish my points,
even if I bend your senses,
when I am this soft.

The spoon is small,
the cup, generous,
the saucer extra absorbent—

past story, beyond end,
like a certain kind
of woman I have been with,
and been.

Tell Our Mothers We Tell Ourselves the Story We Believe Is Ours

1

The women created
the tunnels and the caves
for everyone.

Offering home or a place to hide,
space to be. To be held or hid
or helped to become old.

Blue stone, in nature,
is a trick of the eye,
a sky-trick, light playing air,

sky-diving into earth
to make you see it,
even if it's not there.

2

'Now Dad's gone you can have fun.'

'I could learn to have fun,
but I might never succeed,
and it seems like a waste of whatever
else I could l have a chance to learn.'

'Like puzzles? A new language?'

'Fun doesn't have to be learned
at all if you have it young enough.
But me—I'd have to work at it.
I don't know how to have fun.'

She said that
as if someone else had said it to her.

3

So I said: 'Who told you
you 'don't know how to have fun?'

'What?'

'You said 'One problem with me
is I don't know how to have fun,'

Did someone tell you that about yourself
or is that your own self-knowledge?'

'I think someone told me: you don't know
how to have fun

and I'd never thought about it before: fun.
My life was never fun.

I was a child and children have fun but
not me. Nobody looked after me
and I didn't even have the basics—
not enough was all I knew.

So when someone (your dad) told me
I didn't know 'how to have fun' of course
I believed him.

It was true. That's how I came to believe it,
I think, because of the truth of it. And also because
your dad said it was true.'

But it can't be both.
But it can't be separated.

If you do not copy this letter and mail it to six of your closest
heart-friends (who adore you and think you'd have better judgment
than to do this) you will experience radical misfortune that looks
like fun/luck, (not the sad event that nevertheless yields a golden
river dawn.) The following is just an example:

When the ceiling drops
the rain stops
beating down but
now you're beaten down

though it's the beat
that drops now
and we dance
in the rain
like sunbeams
made out of metal cloth,
tubes of blood,
and scared, sewn-up eyes.

5

Then Dad left—
well.... did he actually leave?

When he was with us he was intensely absent,
But when he physically left it seemed
he was effortlessly still there, still   'with us?'

There must be a difference,
and it can't be both
since one is fact (he left)
and one is fiction. (he's here)

One is an act
and one is addiction.

6

A story of how we travel   (because we want to or need to, rarely both.)

from painful lost-in-the unknown (are *you* my mother?)

and being left out   (in the rain, of the circle, to rot.)

to finding love   (which includes endlessly more
                                             than what's contained by the word of it
                                             but that container holds the map to find it.)

to finding love within   (the longest journey has the same repeating
                                             terrain—switchbacks, backtracks, circles—
                                             only to end up mere paces from the start.)

to making the world without   (is a magic. to imagine and to wonder
reflect the world within   fiercely, is *this* what we're meant to do
                                             in this life?)

and vice versa   (or is there something else?
                                             or is this only for artists?)

to heal both   (is *this* what we're meant to do
entry and exit wounds   in this life?)
to repair the path between

but what if the path remains
broken, the wounds open

and the world wasn't reflected
either to or from itself

neither made nor made of

and we didn't find love within
and we didn't find love
and we weren't left out
so we didn't feel lost and alone

so we never traveled
but stayed here,
whether we wanted to
or needed to   (does that difference make all the
                                                               difference?)

to try to find our true story.   (which may be nowhere, it's true.)

        7

Oh but what is the story, after all that?
it's not a straight line or a jagged one.

It's a spray cloud,
        fast water hitting rock hard
        and exploding,
        then coming together to
        settle back and go
        the original direction
        toward the sea.

The story is many spray clouds
                        and storm clouds
                                wind storms, the breath of trees
                                and other living things, off-gassing.
Clouds of natural gas.
Hot air. Cool breeze. Naturally. Unnaturally.

                                But nothing's natural.
                                And nothing's unnatural either.
                                The original concept is off.
                                Switched off.

Switch it on: that story is winding
both ways,
a short story that's taking forever.

8

The story is a family
of inside and outside,

who begat grass underfoot
and green recycled siding,

who adopted wind energy
and gas guzzling. And invasive
species married in—

and winter vegetables
divorced out.

The heat and the cold grew up
unsupervised, basically, and can't
feel anything.

The flowers so automatically
attached themselves to your leg
as you try to run away

to find another shelter
you can afford
where, if time turns out
to be a good roommate,
you won't have to immediately
make plans to move again,

a thing that's called 'to stay'.

If we keep saying it,
the story might stay   (if it doesn't turn away from us)
and make its home in us,
will travel with us,   (unravel us)
will begin to understand
the family of itself
as it is delivered to us   (living in a grotto, moving to a cave,
as we are delivered to it.   through a tunnel a woman made.)

9

Women cupped their hands
to make baskets
to catch babies
to carry and carry.

Women made the vessels
the tub the cup the jug
the mug, many things
with U in it, held by her
making and making.

Women made the jars
and pitchers to pour
themselves into,
to pour for you,
pouring and pouring
for everyone.

10

The story is a rage/range
of hills and mountains,
—anger dispersed over years
years ago—

that look and feel like a reclining
woman and nobody is offended
by this anymore.

Resting in middle age for energy
to make everything for everybody,
shortly, longingly.

She's the main character even though
she doesn't travel.

She is the traveled.

Who Sings Whose Songs?

(after Torkwase Dyson's 'Sing')

Who will decide once and for all: half empty or half full?

Will it be left to the artist—(is it right for an artist? Is it the right of an artist?) to weigh and lay to rest the question of half, of division, of border, of definition, of edge?

Is that the artist's realm? That power, that naming force: semi is a half-curl, hemi is a cup, demi a reduction.
But half of an infinite form is more than can ever be drained drunk diminished or determined.

Must we trust the artist to give us perspective, to give us proper proportions?
Ask an artist at the dinner party and put everybody on edge.

It doesn't go over well. Doesn't go down easy.
Leave the table to its surface dimensions, service, salt.

Turn your face, an eclipse in cups, a rim aswim in a stemless wineglass.
I'm glass. See through me.

Drink the moon, your reflection, your bottomless river.
A swarm aswirl as well.

Where else does gravity lead if not to the grave?
Why does water bead up on not wet what can't be bathed?

Who can tell me if this is:

> An architect's drawing of whiskey on spherical ice.

> A cross section of a skipped stone mid-skip?

> A dream of taking a bath.

Whale approach.

You, Just Barely Touching My Arm.

Noted: Tiny triangle of intensity in the corner is actually the aperture,
           and we, the observer, will be in this picture.

Noted: Tiny corner triangle pointing out the way (uppish) to large
           circle half-submerged.

           Too many syllables, too many beats for this thing to sing from
           its Cubist face.

           With eye that closes from the bottom.

How are you holding up?

It makes me feel free, to look at this.

Questions of construct, boundaries, gradations, levels, areas, shapes, tones,
dimensions...

are all worked out for me, who looks freely at the artist's work.

Who decides what displaces who?
When you came in the cup was full
so who sloshed out when you came in
and when did you decide to come
and push who down? How are you holding up?

Precise angles exist already everywhere in this wet air,
each new cup and shelf and ridge/edge/wedge/selvedge
is salvaged

from an eternal original
mined
for usable dimensions.

Lines and curves recognise each other, like long lost.

Populations displace people—once places held space
for people, now only for a populace who can afford popular places—

replacing people with populace & allowing populations
to use places to replace people
& make places impossible to afford
so the people can't possibly return, long lost.

Fingerprints on a glass look inked in blood,

the iron rusting on its own home fluid:

nothing can be kept out for good.

Glass looks slick but its made of:

many small staggered fissures, each little dagger cuts its bit of air

bit your tip like a mosquito, leaving a tiny blue pool under the skin.

How rare is something just entirely itself.
Not even water is.

How rare is something just entirely itself.
Not even water is.

A fingerprint is unique, yes, but now it's used for ID and not its ridges &
whorls, for which there is no standard of beauty.

Everything's used
is different than
everything is of use.

Who makes the call—what is in/what is out—whoever has the most
objective sight line?

The artist's eye sees past vision, past even the notion of vision or the
glimmer of the notion—but gives voice to motion.

Who is on edge, in the drink, sink or swim, waving, draining, drowning,
drawing, setting, settling, sunk?

Who is singing, who sung?

On 'Loss of Feathers' by Ursula von Rydingsvard

The hand had a soft surface with firm, padded hills on one side
and hard longish seawalls on the other. Opening this hand meant
pouring out all the moves that made so many pictures and paintings
—those portraits and portals—and looking at the spout, the route.

Where, on its way, did an idea become a physical object? At what point in
the creative process? When thought became action, was it in the first
moment of action that thought gained a materiality of sorts, a seedliness?

Or does an idea retain the essence of thinker-spirit as long as it's being
thought, thought through, and throughout the making process, and when
the making is finally over, only THEN does the idea, now something more
than just the idea, dump the product itself plus the making process, into
the product itself. The made thing then becoming itself the moment it's
finished.

No that can't be right. It has to be the first, right? Thing becomes thing
as soon as it begins to become itself.

No government criminalises abandoned art projects, even though the
promise or even spark of independent life might be there.

The artist's hand is always open, even if it's holding something. Especially
so.

It has to be. The artist's hand guides the horizon of seeing to the very
edge, overlapping, even layering the way you must to cover something
completely. Feathers cover tightly to keep the line of liquid out, wicking
it away.

Birds can't get their skin wet or something? It's a tight weave—waterproof
like skin is, not like hair, which is about warmth.

Warm skin, cold feathers. Cold weather, warm clothes. New form, old
function.

Decades ago, the much older woman, an artist, took my arm and said 'Look at this strong little arm' and marveled, her hand stroking me fingertip to elbow. I was embarrassed. I thought she was envying my young body.

Many years later, now that I envy my own young body, I realise she wasn't coveting mine but finally claiming her own.

We held hands, looked at each other's. Turned them over and around. Feathery age spots, neater freckles, blue ridges and knuckle dimples, wrist wrinkles that go across. Blood traversing its own known way and never crossing another's.

She said you couldn't be an artist and a mother back then. It was impossible, then suddenly unsure, she said well impossible for her. Being a mother, she never wanted to. Lucky she didn't have to. Her arms were for art. Her hands, her fingers in mine, which would make art deep into a future that was done being hers. That had transferred to me.

The idea becomes art, alive, the moment of conception. The eventual object may only be a pinprick at that moment, and it may never develop. Or it might.

The process of making—dissolving idea into body, body into thing, where thing emerges, made.

That one feather, lost, to the bird, on its many-minded journey, is never missed.

Another feather finds its place. But the art was the only one of its kind. And I continue on into a future which won't be mine the way her hand in mine was mine.

The Artist Jessica Rankin

loves poetry.
I love artists who love poetry
(Dorothea Tanning was another)
because artists know what they
create sounds well beyond the edge
of the visual realm. They know
poetry uses vision from a corner
of the palette, a couple blobs
of paint dipped into for highlights
and shadow. Artists love edging
and spilling over into fresh media,
mesh nets spread to catch them.

Who will tell the capacious, frank,
and po-sexual artist Jessica Rankin
that poetry thinks music contains
the attributes the artist attributes
to poetry? That poetry leans hard
on music so constantly that music
doesn't even notice the parasitic
pressure and sponge anymore.
Music's got better things to do
and is not really in a hurry the way
poetry and art sorta seem to be.

Maybe the dancer Georgina will be
asked to perform yet another task
for another's art. Asked to give her
body's limited editions of breath
and blood, her lifetime's supply.
How relentless to embody another's
creation! How necessary, this vexed
vesseling, voice-over-like: not even
music stands on its own without
instruments, and instruments

need players, players need bodies,
bodies need choreography to move
the music out of its resting place,
unsettle the score.

The score, yes, Paola wrote more
than the staff can handle, so lush
on the page the old idea of an opera
on a plain 4-corner stage grows mold.
She knows who broke the music—
those who chose kill it young rather
than have to learn to hear anew.
I'm thinking the choreographer
Lauren—who is new, who grew up
in my hometown decades after I left—
might have something to say about
the institutions in which all our art's
contained, meted out, cut, maimed.

I'll get blowback for saying that.
People who insist on controlling art
will say this isn't art: good. Ignore it.
Too late. I'm interrupted now, here
—no, you're asking—in the middle
of a poem, why I'm dropping names?
I'll namecheck if I please but, please,
I'll not drop these names. I pick them,
from the artistree to graft onto poetree.
It is, you know, a 'high art' and I am
a poet, classically fancy. Just ask
Jessica. Poetry's still up there,
living light in a high rise, editing
the edifice's artifice. Sky-struck.

This poem is only a net (fish-, ether-)
for the artists gathered here in the way
of poets: cornered in a spiraling room
in case they, in the way of poets,

trip the edge and need a soft place
to land. Here: pulsing cloud pillows
with jackknife for the dancer, silk
hagiography for the choreographer,
true wave via childhood for Paola,
dreamy azure drops and lucent streaks
of aubergine (Dorothea's favorite
word) for the artist Jessica Rankin,
who loves poetry.

The Poets Are Dying

It seems impossible
they seemed immortal.

Where are they going
if not to their next poems?

Poems that, like lives, make do
and make that doing do more—

holding a jolt like a newborn,
a volta turning toward a god-load

of grief dumped from some heaven
where words rain down

and the poet is soaked. Cold
to the bone, we've become. Thick-

headed, death-bedded, heartsick.
Poets. Flowers picked, candles wicked,

forgiving everyone they tricked.

What Have I Done?

I was weak, or strong, depending—not interested in judging it now.

I let myself feel what I felt for a person, opened up my need
like a sentence I'd ever serve—a line never-ending, full of song
the air around me kept, cupped, to my always ear.

Now I must prepare for a soundlessness
to be my true time—I'll lose you to something,

if not to this.

I was foolish, headlong, afraid of having nothing—what's wrong with nothing?

I set myself to making you—a new person, if you died I'd die
just that simple. Aren't we simple? You live I live.
You my baby, my hurt perfect one I live in fear for.

Why did I make you, destroyer?
Honey on the wound but the wound is already clean,

having cut you from me, me from you.

I was insolent, stubborn, had to have my way—where was I going?

In debt, myself, to the accident of love I was born into,
was a criminal of. I owed back my air, my word,
every dog and child and poem and lover.

Who do I submit it all to? Who takes them all—everyone
I love—away, and where but where is away?

I believed. I held on. I thought that meant

I could have them.